AESCHY

THE ORESTEIA

AGAMEMNON

THE LIBATION BEARERS

THE EUMENIDES

PROTEUS (FRAGMENTS)

THE COMPLETE GREEK TRAGEDIES

Edited by David Grene & Richmond Lattimore

THIRD EDITION *Edited by Mark Griffith & Glenn W. Most*

ΛΕＳＣΗＹＬＵＳ ΙΙ

THE ORESTEIA *Translated by Richmond Lattimore*

AGAMEMNON

THE LIBATION BEARERS

THE EUMENIDES

PROTEUS (FRAGMENTS) *Translated by Mark Griffith*

The University of Chicago Press CHICAGO & LONDON

MARK GRIFFITH is professor of classics and of theater, dance, and performance studies at the University of California, Berkeley.

GLENN W. MOST is professor of ancient Greek at the Scuola Normale Superiore at Pisa and a visiting member of the Committee on Social Thought at the University of Chicago.

DAVID GRENE (1913–2002) taught classics for many years at the University of Chicago.

RICHMOND LATTIMORE (1906–1984), professor of Greek at Bryn Mawr College, was a poet and translator best known for his translations of the Greek classics, especially his versions of the *Iliad* and the *Odyssey*.

The University of Chicago Press, Chicago 60637
The University of Chicago Press, Ltd., London
© 2013 by The University of Chicago

Agamemnon © 1947 by Richmond Lattimore,
© 1953, 2013 by the University of Chicago
The Libation Bearers, The Eumenides © 1953, 2013
by the University of Chicago
Proteus © 2013 by the University of Chicago

25 24   12

ISBN-13: 978-0-226-31146-3 (cloth)
ISBN-13: 978-0-226-31147-0 (paper)
ISBN-13: 978-0-226-31148-7 (e-book)
ISBN-10: 0-226-31146-5 (cloth)
ISBN-10: 0-226-31147-3 (paper)
ISBN-10: 0-226-31148-1 (e-book)

Cataloging-in-Publication Data is available from the Library of Congress.

♾ This paper meets the requirements of ANSI/
NISO Z39.48–1992 (Permanence of Paper).

CONTENTS

Editors' Preface to the Third Edition · vii

Introduction to Aeschylus · 1

How the Plays Were Originally Staged · 7

THE ORESTEIA: Introduction · 13

AGAMEMNON · 21

THE LIBATION BEARERS · 81

THE EUMENIDES · 123

PROTEUS (FRAGMENTS) · 163

Textual Notes · 167

Glossary · 171

EDITORS' PREFACE TO THE THIRD EDITION

The first edition of the *Complete Greek Tragedies*, edited by David Grene and Richmond Lattimore, was published by the University of Chicago Press starting in 1953. But the origins of the series go back even further. David Grene had already published his translation of three of the tragedies with the same press in 1942, and some of the other translations that eventually formed part of the Chicago series had appeared even earlier. A second edition of the series, with new translations of several plays and other changes, was published in 1991. For well over six decades, these translations have proved to be extraordinarily popular and resilient, thanks to their combination of accuracy, poetic immediacy, and clarity of presentation. They have guided hundreds of thousands of teachers, students, and other readers toward a reliable understanding of the surviving masterpieces of the three great Athenian tragedians: Aeschylus, Sophocles, and Euripides.

But the world changes, perhaps never more rapidly than in the past half century, and whatever outlasts the day of its appearance must eventually come to terms with circumstances very different from those that prevailed at its inception. During this same period, scholarly understanding of Greek tragedy has undergone significant development, and there have been marked changes not only in the readers to whom this series is addressed, but also in the ways in which these texts are taught and studied in universities. These changes have prompted the University of Chicago Press to perform another, more systematic revision of the translations, and we are honored to have been entrusted with this delicate and important task.

Our aim in this third edition has been to preserve and strengthen as far as possible all those features that have made the Chicago translations successful for such a long time, while at the same time revising the texts carefully and tactfully to bring them up to date and equipping them with various kinds of subsidiary help, so they may continue to serve new generations of readers.

Our revisions have addressed the following issues:

- Wherever possible, we have kept the existing translations. But we have revised them where we found this to be necessary in order to bring them closer to the ancient Greek of the original texts or to replace an English idiom that has by now become antiquated or obscure. At the same time we have done our utmost to respect the original translator's individual style and meter.

- In a few cases, we have decided to substitute entirely new translations for the ones that were published in earlier editions of the series. Euripides' *Medea* has been newly translated by Oliver Taplin, *The Children of Heracles* by Mark Griffith, *Andromache* by Deborah Roberts, and *Iphigenia among the Taurians* by Anne Carson. We have also, in the case of Aeschylus, added translations and brief discussions of the fragments of lost plays that originally belonged to connected tetralogies along with the surviving tragedies, since awareness of these other lost plays is often crucial to the interpretation of the surviving ones. And in the case of Sophocles, we have included a translation of the substantial fragmentary remains of one of his satyr-dramas, *The Trackers* (*Ichneutai*). (See "How the Plays Were Originally Staged" below for explanation of "tetralogy," "satyr-drama," and other terms.)

- We have altered the distribution of the plays among the various volumes in order to reflect the chronological order in which they were written, when this is known or can be estimated with some probability. Thus the *Oresteia* appears now as volume 2 of Aeschylus' tragedies, and the sequence of Euripides' plays has been rearranged.

- We have rewritten the stage directions to make them more consistent throughout, keeping in mind current scholarly understanding of how Greek tragedies were staged in the fifth century BCE. In general, we have refrained from extensive stage directions of an interpretive kind, since these are necessarily speculative and modern scholars often disagree greatly about them. The Greek manuscripts themselves contain no stage directions at all.

- We have indicated certain fundamental differences in the meters and modes of delivery of all the verse of these plays. Spoken language (a kind of heightened ordinary speech, usually in the iambic trimeter rhythm) in which the characters of tragedy regularly engage in dialogue and monologue is printed in ordinary Roman font; the sung verse of choral and individual lyric odes (using a large variety of different meters), and the chanted verse recited by the chorus or individual characters (always using the anapestic meter), are rendered in *italics*, with parentheses added where necessary to indicate whether the passage is sung or chanted. In this way, readers will be able to tell at a glance how the playwright intended a given passage to be delivered in the theater, and how these shifting dynamics of poetic register contribute to the overall dramatic effect.

- All the Greek tragedies that survive alternate scenes of action or dialogue, in which individual actors speak all the lines, with formal songs performed by the chorus. Occasionally individual characters sing formal songs too, or they and the chorus may alternate lyrics and spoken verse within the same scene. Most of the formal songs are structured as a series of pairs of stanzas of which the metrical form of the first one ("strophe") is repeated exactly by a second one ("antistrophe"). Thus the metrical structure will be, e.g., strophe A, antistrophe A, strophe B, antistrophe B, with each pair of stanzas consisting of a different sequence of rhythms. Occasionally a short stanza in a different metrical form ("mesode") is inserted in the middle between one strophe and the corresponding antistrophe, and sometimes the end of the whole series is marked with a single stanza in a different metrical form ("epode")—thus, e.g., strophe A, mesode, antistrophe A; or strophe A, antistrophe A, strophe B, antistrophe B, epode. We have indicated these metrical structures by inserting the terms

STROPHE, ANTISTROPHE, MESODE, and EPODE above the first line of the relevant stanzas so that readers can easily recognize the compositional structure of these songs.

- In each play we have indicated by the symbol ° those lines or words for which there are significant uncertainties regarding the transmitted text, and we have explained as simply as possible in textual notes at the end of the volume just what the nature and degree of those uncertainties are. These notes are not at all intended to provide anything like a full scholarly apparatus of textual variants, but instead to make readers aware of places where the text transmitted by the manuscripts may not exactly reflect the poet's own words, or where the interpretation of those words is seriously in doubt.
- For each play we have provided a brief introduction that gives essential information about the first production of the tragedy, the mythical or historical background of its plot, and its reception in antiquity and thereafter.
- For each of the three great tragedians we have provided an introduction to his life and work. It is reproduced at the beginning of each volume containing his tragedies.
- We have also provided at the end of each volume a glossary explaining the names of all persons and geographical features that are mentioned in any of the plays in that volume.

It is our hope that our work will help ensure that these translations continue to delight, to move, to astonish, to disturb, and to instruct many new readers in coming generations.

MARK GRIFFITH, *Berkeley*
GLENN W. MOST, *Florence*

INTRODUCTION TO AESCHYLUS

Aeschylus was born sometime in the 520s BCE into an aristocratic family based in Eleusis, twelve miles to the west of central Athens. So he was a teenager when the ruling monarchical family of the Pisistratids was expelled and the first democracy at Athens was created (510-508). As well as becoming the greatest tragic playwright of his generation, Aeschylus fought against the Persians at Marathon (490), where his brother was killed, and in the sea battle at Salamis (480). He began producing plays in the 490s, won his first victory in 484, and continued writing tragedies until shortly before his death in 455. The epitaph that was written on Aeschylus' tomb (in Gela, Sicily)—allegedly composed by him and his family—mentions his service at Marathon against the Persians, but says nothing about his achievement as a playwright.

The titles of over ninety plays by Aeschylus are recorded, though only six survive that can be attributed to him with certainty (scholars are divided about the authenticity of the *Prometheus Bound* that is transmitted under his name). On several occasions he composed his plays for the annual competition to be a continuous and coherent sequence, with the three tragedies forming almost a single—very extended—three-act play, as we find with the *Oresteia*. (The fourth play of the sequence was of course a satyr-drama, usually connected thematically to the three preceding tragedies; see p. 7 below.) Unfortunately, we do not possess more than one play from any of Aeschylus' other trilogies; and we possess only small fragments from any of his satyr-plays. Some of Aeschylus' rivals likewise produced connected trilogies: but some did not, preferring to compose three quite separate tragedies on different themes; and sometimes Aeschylus did this too, as in the case of the plays produced with his *Persians* (472). It is striking that Sophocles, who began his playwriting career in 468 BCE and for over a decade was competing against Aeschylus, seems never to have adopted the "connected" trilogy format at all; nor subsequently did Euripides.

Tragedy and satyr-drama were already well established in Athens by the late sixth century, and when Aeschylus began to produce plays he was competing against several famous rivals, most notably Phrynichus, Choerilus, and Pratinas. Almost nothing of their work survives, so it is impossible to gauge to what point the art of tragedy had advanced before Aeschylus. Some scholars have regarded him as being effectively the "creator" of Greek tragedy, but it is clear that his predecessors and rivals were highly regarded, especially for their music and choral song, and the fact that he seems to us to be such a powerful innovator may be due in part to the loss of his rivals' works. In any case, Aeschylus undoubtedly played a major role in developing tragedy to its pinnacle of dramatic sophistication and moral power, and he established himself as by far the most popular and influential of all the tragedians before Sophocles, winning thirteen first prizes in the years between 484 and 458.

Aeschylus' unique tragic style is especially remarkable for its extensive and intensive use of the chorus: some of the choral songs extend for over 150 lines each, and the variety of meters and complexity of structure and language are astonishing. His language too is bold and unconventional, with extensive use of metaphor and imagery. Aeschylus was credited by some with introducing the second speaking actor, and possibly also (late in his career) the third (though some ancient critics credited this to the young Sophocles). Another innovative move of his was to cast the chorus as leading characters in certain plays (for example, *The Suppliant Maidens* and *The Eumenides*). He also seems to have been among the first to have taken dramatic advantage of the *skênê* building: the *Oresteia* is the first surviving drama to contain scenes that require three speaking actors on stage simultaneously; and the positioning of the Watchman on the roof in *Agamemnon*, and the frequent references throughout the trilogy to the "door" and to entrances in and out of the "house" or "temple," are unprecedented in earlier plays.

Aeschylus is said to have visited Sicily at some point during the 470s as the guest of Hieron, ruler of Syracuse and Acragas, and to have composed and presented plays there. But he appears to have been resident in Athens for most of the rest of his life, producing plays about Achilles and Patroclus, about Pentheus and Dionysus, about Niobe, about Ajax, Philoctetes, and the death of Hector (all themes popular also with later tragedians), and others too, in addition to those trilogies of which parts or all survive to the present: *The Seven against Thebes* (467), *The Suppliant Maidens* (probably 463), and his masterwork, the *Oresteia* (458). The date, and even the authenticity, of the Prometheus trilogy (of which *Prometheus Bound* survives complete, as well as several fragments of *Prometheus Unbound*) are very uncertain: these issues are discussed further in the introduction to that play. Within a year of producing the *Oresteia*, Aeschylus left Athens for another visit to Sicily, and died there in 456 or 455.

We know nothing about the personality or lifestyle of Aeschylus, though we do know that one of his sons, Euaion, was a renowned beauty, as well as being a playwright and actor of distinction. The other son, Euphorion, was also a very successful tragedian, and the family continued to flourish in the world of Athenian theater throughout the fifth and fourth centuries. Aristotle and other ancient sources report that Aeschylus was an initiate of the Eleusinian Mysteries in honor of the goddesses Demeter and Persephone, and that he was once prosecuted for revealing secret aspects of the Eleusinian Mysteries in one of his plays—but was acquitted. Scholars both ancient and modern, while viewing such stories with some degree of skepticism (since ancient "biographies" of poets tend to be wildly fanciful and unreliable), have generally agreed that Aeschylus' plays consistently display a serious and challenging engagement with religious matters, though they disagree as to whether specifically Eleusinian and eschato-logical elements can be identified.

After his death, Aeschylus' reputation continued to flourish. His sons doubtless helped to keep his plays in the public eye; and an ancient tradition (perhaps not trustworthy) states that the Athenians passed a special decree allowing Aeschylus' plays to be revived at the annual festival, an honor granted to no other deceased playwright. One way or another, some of his plays clearly did continue to be performed and to be read, at least by the highly educated, since allusions and parodies are frequently found in the plays of Euripides and Aristophanes. When Aristophanes came to write the *Frogs*, shortly after the death of Euripides in 405, he presented the clash between old and new tragedy as a contest between Aeschylus and Euripides. In the quotations and parodies that abound in that comedy, Aeschylus' style is consistently represented as being "grandiloquent," high-flown to the point of obscurity or bombast, and geared to maintaining the dignity and solemnity of the tragic genre, as against Euripides' modernizing tendencies and introduction of more everyday issues, unpoetic language, and low characters.

During the fourth century, Aeschylus' plays, along with those of Sophocles and Euripides but no other Athenian tragedians, were acknowledged as classics and as being especially worthy of being preserved and performed—though it seems that by this date there was little concern for keeping whole trilogies together (plays instead were catalogued alphabetically), and also a diminishing interest in satyr-plays. A more or less complete collection of Aeschylus' plays was made in Alexandria during the third century BCE, and even though Aeschylus' plays were generally regarded as being less accessible and enjoyable than Sophocles' and especially Euripides'—because of Aeschylus' more archaic language, large amounts of choral lyric, and limited opportunities for actors and rhetoricians to exploit the argumentative and ethical dimensions of the characters' speeches—all three tragedians were read in both Greek and Roman schools throughout antiquity.

Scores of fragments from Aeschylus' plays, mostly quite short, are found in quotations by other authors and in anthologies from the period between the third century BCE and the fourth century CE; but they are far fewer and less extensive than the fragments of Sophocles or (especially) Euripides; and the same is true of papyrus finds. So while Aeschylus remained a classic both in the schools and among later practitioners of the dramatic art (including Ennius, Accius, Pacuvius, and Seneca in Rome), familiarity with his work at first hand seems to have become increasingly limited, even in the schools. Some of his plays certainly were much better known than others, and the selection of seven plays that we possess was probably made in the second century CE: from that point on, the other plays ceased to be copied and thus eventually were lost to posterity. At Byzantium (Constantinople, today Istanbul), three plays in particular were most widely copied, the triad consisting of *Prometheus Bound, The Seven against Thebes*, and *The Persians*. The other four plays fell into almost complete neglect, and two of them (*The Suppliant Maidens* and *The Libation Bearers*) are preserved in only one manuscript copy. It is sobering to realize that without this one manuscript, we would not possess the complete *Oresteia* trilogy.

Aeschylus' reputation in the modern era has rested almost entirely on the seven plays that survive in our medieval manuscripts. During the Renaissance and Enlightenment periods, his plays were still relatively little read and seldom performed. Things changed when German and British Romantic poets and intellectuals of the eighteenth and nineteenth centuries began to pay more attention to archaic Greek literature and to aspects of Hellenic culture that had for long been regarded as "primitive" or crude. Aeschylus became the object of increasing admiration and study, for his arresting and large-scale religious questioning, his powerful presentation of moral and political problems, his musical and ritualistic energy, and his sheer linguistic exuberance and density. Since the nineteenth century, indeed, his plays have been regarded as the foundation stones of Western drama. The *Oresteia* has always been by far the most widely read and often staged, though *Prometheus Bound* has also been influential with progressives and revolutionaries of various hues. Aeschylus' reputation continued to grow throughout the twentieth century, especially because of his challenging representation of gender conflict and sociopolitical crisis; his plays have been more widely read and staged, decade by decade, and nowadays he stands unchallenged as the true "father of Greek tragedy."

HOW THE PLAYS WERE ORIGINALLY STAGED

Nearly all the plays composed by Aeschylus, Sophocles, and Euripides were first performed in the Theater of Dionysus at Athens, as part of the annual festival and competition in drama. This was not only a literary and musical event, but also an important religious and political ceremony for the Athenian community. Each year three tragedians were selected to compete, with each of them presenting four plays per day, a "tetralogy" of three tragedies and one satyr-play. The satyr-play was a type of drama similar to tragedy in being based on heroic myth and employing many of the same stylistic features, but distinguished by having a chorus of half-human, half-horse followers of Dionysus—sileni or satyrs—and by always ending happily. Extant examples of this genre are Euripides' *The Cyclops* (in *Euripides*, vol. 5) and Sophocles' *The Trackers* (partially preserved: in *Sophocles*, vol. 2).

The three competing tragedians were ranked by a panel of citizens functioning as amateur judges, and the winner received an honorific prize. Records of these competitions were maintained, allowing Aristotle and others later to compile lists of the dates when each of Aeschylus', Sophocles', and Euripides' plays were first performed and whether they placed first, second, or third in the competition (unfortunately we no longer possess the complete lists).

The tragedians competed on equal terms: each had at his disposal three actors (only two in Aeschylus' and in Euripides' earliest plays) who would often have to switch between roles as each play progressed, plus other nonspeaking actors to play attendants and other subsidiary characters; a chorus of twelve (in Aeschylus'

time) or fifteen (for most of the careers of Sophocles and Euripides), who would sing and dance formal songs and whose Chorus Leader would engage in dialogue with the characters or offer
comment on the action; and a pipe-player, to accompany the
sung portions of the play.

All the performers were men, and the actors and chorus members all wore masks. The association of masks with other Diony-
sian rituals may have affected their use in the theater; but masks
had certain practical advantages as well—for example, making
it easy to play female characters and to change quickly between
roles. In general, the use of masks also meant that ancient acting techniques must have been rather different from what we are
used to seeing in the modern theater. Acting in a mask requires
a more frontal and presentational style of performance toward
the audience than is usual with unmasked, "realistic" acting; a
masked actor must communicate far more by voice and stylized
bodily gesture than by facial expression, and the gradual development of a character in the course of a play could hardly be indicated by changes in his or her mask. Unfortunately, however, we
know almost nothing about the acting techniques of the Athenian theater. But we do know that the chorus members were all
Athenian amateurs, and so were the actors up until the later part
of the fifth century, by which point a prize for the best actor had
been instituted in the tragic competition, and the art of acting
(which of course included solo singing and dancing) was becoming increasingly professionalized.

The tragedian himself not only wrote the words for his play
but also composed the music and choreography and directed the
productions. It was said that Aeschylus also acted in his plays but
that Sophocles chose not to, except early in his career, because
his voice was too weak. Euripides is reported to have had a col-
laborator who specialized in musical composition. The costs for
each playwright's production were shared between an individual
wealthy citizen, as a kind of "super-tax" requirement, and the city.

The Theater of Dionysus itself during most of the fifth century BCE probably consisted of a large rectangular or trapezoidal

dance floor, backed by a one-story wooden building (the *skênê*), with a large central door that opened onto the dance floor. (Some scholars have argued that two doors were used, but the evidence is thin.) Between the *skênê* and the dance floor there may have been a narrow stage on which the characters acted and which communicated easily with the dance floor. For any particular play, the *skênê* might represent a palace, a house, a temple, or a cave, for example; the interior of this "building" was generally invisible to the audience, with all the action staged in front of it. Sophocles is said to have been the first to use painted scenery; this must have been fairly simple and easy to remove, as every play had a different setting. Playwrights did not include stage directions in their texts. Instead, a play's setting was indicated explicitly by the speaking characters.

All the plays were performed in the open air and in daylight. Spectators sat on wooden seats in rows, probably arranged in rectangular blocks along the curving slope of the Acropolis. (The stone semicircular remains of the Theater of Dionysus that are visible today in Athens belong to a later era.) Seating capacity seems to have been four to six thousand—thus a mass audience, but not quite on the scale of the theaters that came to be built during the fourth century BCE and later at Epidaurus, Ephesus, and many other locations all over the Mediterranean.

Alongside the *skênê*, on each side, there were passages through which actors could enter and exit. The acting area included the dance floor, the doorway, and the area immediately in front of the *skênê*. Occasionally an actor appeared on the roof or above it, as if flying. He was actually hanging from a crane (*mêchanê*: hence *deus ex machina*, "a god from the machine"). The *skênê* was also occasionally opened up—the mechanical details are uncertain—in order to show the audience what was concealed within (usually dead bodies). Announcements of entrances and exits, like the setting, were made by the characters. Although the medieval manuscripts of the surviving plays do not provide explicit stage directions, it is usually possible to infer from the words or from the context whether a particular entrance or exit is being made through a door (into the *skênê*) or by one of the side entrances. In later antiquity, there may have been a rule that one side entrance always led to the city center, the other to the countryside or harbor. Whether such a rule was ever observed in the fifth century is uncertain.

THE ORESTEIA

Translated by RICHMOND LATTIMORE

THE ORESTEIA: INTRODUCTION

The Plays: Date and Composition

Aeschylus' most famous and perennially successful masterpiece, the tetralogy of plays comprising *Agamemnon*, *The Libation Bearers* (in Greek, *Choephoroi*), *The Eumenides*, and the satyr-drama *Proteus*, won first prize in the Athenian tragedy competition of 458 BCE. The three tragedies are the only connected trilogy to have survived from antiquity. We do not know when the title *Oresteia* for the whole group was first assigned, but we find *The Libation Bearers* being referred to individually as "The Oresteia" in Aristophanes' *Frogs*. The three tragedies later came to be listed separately (in alphabetical order) among the plays of Aeschylus, and seem most often to have been read separately too. We cannot tell how often the whole trilogy was performed after its initial production; but some ancient readers certainly knew the sequence of plays, and it cannot be mere accident that these three tragedies were included among the seven that were preserved in our medieval manuscript tradition.

The Myth

The sequence of calamities and grisly deeds of vengeance within the family of Tantalus was a common subject of poetic narratives and dramas in antiquity; likewise the saga of tales about the Trojan War and its aftermath. Aeschylus wove together several elements from both of these traditions to make his complex yet tightly connected tetralogy. The most important are the following.

Tantalus' son Pelops had two sons, Atreus and Thyestes. They squabbled about the inheritance and throne. In pursuit of his ambitions, Thyestes seduced Atreus' wife, but Atreus got his revenge by pretending to seek reconciliation, inviting his brother to dinner, and there serving him his own (Thyestes') children to eat, chopped into pieces and cooked in a stew. When Thyestes realized what had happened he pronounced a curse on Atreus and all his descendants.

After some years had passed, Atreus' two sons, Agamemnon and Menelaus, became the kings of Mycenae/Argos and Sparta, respectively—though sometimes they are described in the *Oresteia* as being still a united pair, "the Atreidae," both of them apparently residing in the "House of Atreus." They were married to the two daughters of King Tyndareus of Sparta, Clytaemestra (sometimes spelled Clytemnestra) and Helen.

Meanwhile, Thyestes' one surviving son, Aegisthus (cousin of Agamemnon and Menelaus), was growing up separately, planning vengeance for Atreus' crime against his father.

When the Trojan prince Paris/Alexander, son of King Priam, visited Menelaus and eloped with his wife, Helen, Agamemnon organized a huge Panhellenic expedition to recapture her and punish Paris, Priam, and the whole city of Troy. The expedition assembled at Aulis (on the east coast of mainland Greece), but before it could sail for Troy a favorable wind had to be obtained—which could only be brought about, apparently, through the sacrifice of Iphigeneia (also spelled Iphigenia), the eldest daughter of Agamemnon and Clytaemestra. (In most versions of the myth, the goddess Artemis actually saves Iphigenia at the last moment and substitutes a deer instead, though everyone present still believes the girl has been killed. In the *Oresteia*, such a rescue is neither directly indicated nor explicitly excluded.)

While Agamemnon is away fighting for ten years at Troy, Clytaemestra, bitterly resentful of his killing of their daughter, forms an adulterous relationship with Aegisthus, who is still planning to avenge his father and brothers for Atreus' crime. Together they plot Agamemnon's death. When Agamemnon returns victorious from Troy, bringing with him vast war-spoils and a new Trojan slave concubine, Cassandra, daughter of King

Priam, Clytaemestra welcomes him and lures him into the palace, where, with Aegisthus' help, she kills him and Cassandra. They take control of Argos/Mycenae and become rulers—what the Greeks would call "tyrants," or nonhereditary kings. So ends the first play, *Agamemnon*.

Several years later, Orestes, the son of Agamemnon and Clytaemestra, who as a child was not present at the killing of his father and has grown up in Phocis (near Delphi) as the ward of Strophius and his son Pylades, consults with the god Apollo at Delphi and is told that he must seek vengeance for his father's murder. He returns to Argos, accompanied by Pylades, is reunited with his sister Electra, and successfully carries out his long-awaited revenge, killing Aegisthus and Clytaemestra and thus regaining his kingdom and inheritance. At this point, the avenging spirits, or curses, of his mother (in Greek, *Erinyes*) begin to hound him, and he flees in a state of acute mental disturbance. Here ends the second play, *The Libation Bearers*.

Orestes goes to Delphi for purification of the matricidal blood, and Apollo continues to protect him against the Furies. But they persist in pursuing and tormenting him, and eventually some kind of resolution has to be found. In Aeschylus' version, this takes place in Athens when a trial is held before the Court of the Areopagus, with Athena herself presiding.

The Areopagus Council was a venerable Athenian institution, composed of former archons—high-ranking elected officials. In the years just before the first production of the *Oresteia*, amid bitter civic dissension, new reforms had been enacted by the democracy, removing many of the council's powers but leaving it with its traditional responsibility for homicide trials. The idea of having the Argive hero Orestes come to Athens and be prosecuted in front of the Areopagus Court may or may not be Aeschylus' own invention: scholars disagree. In the trial, the Furies are the prosecutors, Apollo the defense counsel. As the result of an evenly split vote, Orestes is acquitted, and Athena, through her great patience and tact, manages to persuade the Furies not to punish the city of Athens for its leniency toward a matricide but to accept instead a position of honor for themselves within the city: they are to become the "august goddesses" who will live in the caves below the Acropolis and will protect the city in the future from all kinds of ills. Thus *The Eumenides*—and the trilogy—comes to an end. (Alas, we know little about how the fourth play proceeded, the satyr-drama *Proteus*; but see pp. 165–66.)

Most of the elements in this saga were already familiar to Aeschylus' Athenian audience. Homer's *Odyssey* was especially important for the pointed parallels and contrasts drawn between Orestes and Telemachus, Aegisthus and the suitors, Clytaemestra and Penelope—though the actual matricide is not explicitly mentioned, and no ugly consequences for Orestes' vengeance seem even to be implied. Important too was the epic poem from the Trojan Cycle titled *Returns* (*Nostoi*), ascribed to Homer; but this is now lost and we do not know how it treated Agamemnon's death and Orestes' vengeance. Many other poetic and visual treatments were in circulation, including perhaps Pindar's eleventh Pythian ode (scholars disagree whether that poem was composed before or after the *Oresteia*). Vase paintings and sculptures of the sixth and early fifth centuries tend to focus on the killing of Aegisthus, not of Clytaemestra, and thus give the vengeance a complexion very different from Aeschylus'. The most influential "source" for Aeschylus seems to have been Stesichorus' choral lyric poetry (from sixth-century Sicily), which appears to have dwelt quite vividly on the troubling issues of matricide, including descriptions of Clytaemestra dreaming about a snake, a prominent Nurse character, and vengeful Furies pursuing Orestes so that Apollo has to intervene. Surviving fragments of Stesichorus' poems on this theme also show that, like Aeschylus in *The Libation Bearers*, he included a recognition scene between Orestes and Electra involving a lock of hair.

Whether other Athenian playwrights before Aeschylus had handled this story we do not know. Probably. But it is likely he was the first to draw together so many strands of the Agamemnon-Clytaemestra-Aegisthus-Helen-Orestes-Electra-Furies story into a trilogy, together with such a rich assortment of events and personalities from the Trojan War; and likely too that it was his innovation to have Orestes come to Athens and be tried before the Areopagus council, with Apollo, the Furies, and Athena all in court together. The masterstroke of a chorus composed of Furies is likely also to have been new, and surprising.

Transmission and Reception

The *Oresteia* was immediately very successful and influential. Numerous other Athenian playwrights revisited parts of this story, often alluding more or less openly to Aeschylus' treatment, and sometimes deliberately, even flamboyantly, diverging from his version of the events. Among surviving plays, Euripides' *Electra*, *Iphigenia among the Taurians*, *Orestes*, and *Iphigenia at Aulis* all owe obvious debts to the *Oresteia*, as does Sophocles' *Electra*. Athenian red-figure vase painters, and in due course south Italian painters as well, were likewise familiar with the trilogy: especially popular were scenes depicting the death of Cassandra; the meeting at Agamemnon's tomb of Orestes and Pylades, wearing travelers' clothes, with Electra and her jug of libations; and the pursuit of Orestes by the Furies and Apollo's protection of him at Delphi. In later years, depictions of the madness of Orestes became a common feature too, though these were generally based more on Euripides' versions than on Aeschylus'.

In later Greek and Roman literature and art, all these themes continued to be well known and frequently adapted. But it is generally hard to identify particular debts to the *Oresteia* rather than to the *Electra* plays of Sophocles and Euripides, both of which were very popular, or to Euripides' enormously successful *Orestes*. Roman playwrights under the Republic (Ennius, Pacuvius, Accius) all composed plays on parts of this story, though these do not survive; and Seneca's *Thyestes* and *Agamemnon*, composed in the first century CE, both became extremely influential on Elizabethan English dramatists as well as on neoclassical French and Italian writers and painters.

While it is impossible to assess how often the *Oresteia* or indi-

vidual plays from it were performed in the centuries between Aeschylus' death and the Renaissance, these were certainly among
the better known of Aeschylus' dramas, and were included in the
Greek and Roman school curriculum, though it looks as if awareness of the satyr-play, *Proteus*, faded out of the picture relatively
early. In later antiquity, the selection of seven Aeschylean tragedies (perhaps for school use) included all three parts of the *Oresteia*, which might indicate that the trilogy was still recognized as a
unity. These seven plays survived—barely—to form our medieval
manuscript tradition of Aeschylus; but by the tenth century copy-
ists had apparently ceased to pay attention to the trilogic connec-
tions, and *The Libation Bearers* in particular fell out of general circulation. Only a single manuscript (the famous Mediceus, which
ended up in the library of Lorenzo Medici in Florence) preserves
this play; and even in this the opening lines are lost.

Since the nineteenth century, the almost cosmic scale of the
Oresteia, its ritualistic and religious qualities, its progressive
moral and political "message" focusing on the transition from
family vendetta to legal process, and its sheer poetic, dramatic,
and visual brilliance have ensured that it is frequently performed
(sometimes *Agamemnon* alone, but often all three plays) and con-
stantly adapted by modern writers and visual artists. Indeed, it is
universally regarded not only by historians of theater but also by
philosophers, political theorists, and literary critics as one of the
greatest masterpieces of Western culture. The German operatic
composer Richard Wagner's notion of a *Gesamtkunstwerk* ("total
work of theater art"), as well as his deployment of recurrent *leit-
motivs*, drew heavily from his reading of the *Oresteia* and its dense
systems of verbal and visual imagery. More recently, the stark and
pervasive gender politics of the trilogy have also provoked con-
tinuing attention and discussion.

Translators, playwrights, and adapters who have tackled all or
part of the *Oresteia* include Robert Browning (1877); Robinson Jef-
fers, *The Tower beyond Tragedy* (1924, revised 1950); Eugene O'Neill,
Mourning Becomes Electra (1931); Jean-Paul Sartre, *Les Mouches* [*The
Flies*] (1943); Tony Harrison (1981). Particularly distinguished

modern stage productions of the trilogy, entire or adapted, include those by Max Reinhardt (1911), Martha Graham (*Clytemnestra*, 1958), Tyrone Guthrie (1967), Karolos Koun with the Theatro Technis (Epidaurus, 1980), Peter Stein (Berlin, 1980), the National Theater of Great Britain (1981, translated by Tony Harrison; directed by Peter Hall), Ariane Mnouchkine with Le Théâtre du Soleil (*Les Atrides*, 1991, translated by Hélène Cixous), and Yael Farber (*Molora*, South Africa, 2011).

AGAMEMNON

Characters   WATCHMAN
          CHORUS of Argive Elders
          CLYTAEMESTRA, wife of Agamemnon
          HERALD
          AGAMEMNON, son of Atreus and king of Argos
          CASSANDRA, daughter of King Priam of Troy
          AEGISTHUS, cousin of Agamemnon

Scene: Argos, in front of the palace of King Agamemnon. The Watchman is posted on the roof.

WATCHMAN

I ask the gods some respite from the weariness
of this watchtime measured by years I lie awake
elbowed upon the Atreidae's roof dogwise to mark
the grand processionals of all the stars of night
burdened with winter and again with heat for men,   5
dynasties in their shining blazoned on the air,
these stars, upon their wane and when the rest arise.
I wait; to read the meaning in that beacon light,
a blaze of fire to carry out of Troy the rumor
and outcry of its capture; to such end a lady's   10
male strength of heart in its high confidence ordains.
Now as this bed stricken with night and drenched with dew
I keep, nor ever with kind dreams for company—
since fear in sleep's place stands forever at my head
against strong closure of my eyes, or any rest—   15

I mince such medicine against sleep failed: I sing,
only to weep again the pity of this house
no longer, as once, administered in the grand way.
Now let there be again redemption from distress,
the flare burning from the blackness in good augury.   20

(A light shows in the distance.)

Oh hail, blaze of the darkness, harbinger of day's
shining, and of processionals and dance and songs
of multitudes in Argos for this day of thanks.
Ho there, ho!
I cry the news aloud to Agamemnon's queen,   25
that she may rise up from her bed of state with speed
to raise the rumor of gladness welcoming this beacon,
and singing rise, if truly the citadel of Ilium
has fallen, as the shining of this flare proclaims.
I also, I, will make my choral prelude, since   30
my lord's dice cast aright are counted as my own,
and mine the tripled sixes of this torchlit throw.
May it only happen. May my king come home, and I
take up within this hand the hand I love. The rest
I leave to silence; for an ox stands huge upon   35
my tongue. The house itself, could it take voice, might speak
aloud and plain. I speak to those who understand,
but if they fail, I have forgotten everything.

(Exit. Enter the Chorus from the side.)

CHORUS [*chanting*]
Ten years since the great contestants   40
of Priam's right,
Menelaus and Agamemnon, my lord,
twin throned, twin sceptered, in twofold power
of kings from god, the Atreidae,
put forth from this shore   45
the thousand ships of the Argives,
the strength and the armies.

Their cry of war went shrill from the heart,
as eagles stricken in agony
for young perished, high from the nest   50
eddy and circle
to bend and sweep of the wings' stroke,
lost far below
the fledglings, the nest, and the tendance.
Yet someone hears in the air, a god,   55
Apollo, Pan, or Zeus, the high
thin wail of these sky-guests, and drives
late to its mark
the Fury upon the transgressors.

So drives Zeus, the great god of guests,   60
the Atreidae against Alexander:
for one woman's promiscuous sake
the struggling masses, legs tired,
knees grinding in dust,
spears broken in the onset.   65
Danaans and Trojans
they have it alike. It goes as it goes
now. The end will be destiny.
You cannot burn flesh or pour unguents,
not innocent cool tears,°   70
that will soften the gods' stiff anger.
But we, dishonored, old in our bones,
cast off even then from the gathering horde,
stay here, to prop up
on staves the strength of a baby.   75
Since the young vigor that urges
inward to the heart
is frail as age, no warcraft yet perfect,
while beyond age, leaf
withered, man goes three-footed   80
no stronger than a child is,
a dream that falters in daylight.°

But you, lady,
daughter of Tyndareus, Clytaemestra, our queen:
What is there to be done? What new thing have you heard?   85
In persuasion of what
report do you order such sacrifice?
To all the gods of the city,
the high and the deep spirits,
to them of the sky and the marketplaces,   90
the altars blaze with oblations.
The staggered flame goes sky-high
one place, then another,
drugged by the simple soft
persuasion of sacred unguents,   95
the deep-stored oil of the kings.
Of these things what can be told
openly, speak.
Be healer to this perplexity
that grows now into darkness of thought,   100
while again sweet hope shining from the flames
beats back the pitiless pondering
of sorrow that eats my heart.

[singing]

STROPHE A

I have mastery yet to proclaim the wonder at the wayside
given to kings. Still by god's grace there surges within me   105
singing magic
grown to my life and power,
how the wild bird portent
hurled forth the Achaeans'
twin-stemmed power single-hearted,   110
lords of the youth of Hellas,
with spear and hand of strength
to the land of Teucrus.
Kings of birds to the kings of the ships,

one black, one blazed with silver,   115
clear seen by the royal house
on the right, the spear hand,
they alighted, watched by all
tore a hare, ripe, bursting with young unborn yet,
stayed from her last fleet running.   120
    Sing sorrow, sorrow: but good win out in the end.

ANTISTROPHE A

Then the grave seer of the host saw through to the hearts divided,
knew the fighting sons of Atreus feeding on the hare
with the host, their people.
Seeing beyond, he spoke: 125
"With time, this foray
shall stalk the city of Priam;
and under the walls, Fate shall spoil
in violence the rich herds of the people.   130
Only let no doom of the gods darken
upon this huge iron forged to curb Troy—
from inward. Artemis the undefiled
is angered with pity
at the flying hounds of her father   135
eating the unborn young in the hare and the shivering mother.
She is sick at the eagles' feasting.
    Sing sorrow, sorrow: but good win out in the end.

EPODE

Lovely she is and kind   140
to the tender young of ravening lions.
For sucklings of all the savage
beasts that lurk in the lonely places she has sympathy.
She demands meaning° for these appearances
good, yet not without evil.   145
Healer Apollo, I pray you
let her not with crosswinds
bind the ships of the Danaans

to time-long anchorage 150
forcing a second sacrifice unholy, untasted,
working bitterness in the blood and fearing no man.
For the terror returns like sickness to lurk in the house;
the secret anger remembers the child that shall be avenged." 155
Such, with great good things beside, rang out in the voice of
    Calchas,
these fatal signs from the birds by the way to the house of the
    princes,
wherewith in sympathy
    sing sorrow, sorrow: but good win out in the end.

Zeus: whatever he may be, if this name 160
pleases him in invocation,
thus I call upon him.
I have pondered everything
yet I cannot find a way,
only Zeus, to cast this dead weight of ignorance 165
finally from out my brain.

He who in time long ago was great,
throbbing with gigantic strength,
shall be as if he never were, unspoken. 170
He who followed him has found
his master, and is gone.
Cry aloud without fear the victory of Zeus;
you will not have failed the truth. 175

Zeus, who guided men to think,
who has laid it down that wisdom
comes alone through suffering.
Still there drips in sleep against the heart
grief of memory; against 180

our will temperance comes.
From the gods who sit in grandeur
grace is somehow violent.

ANTISTROPHE C

On that day the elder king
of the Achaean ships, not faulting
any prophet's word,   185
shifted with the crosswinds of fortune,
when no ship sailed, no pail was full,
and the Achaean people sulked
along the shore at Aulis facing
Chalcis, where tides ebb and surge: 190

STROPHE D

and winds blew from the Strymon, bearing
sick idleness, ships tied fast, and hunger,
distraction of the mind, carelessness
for hull and cable;   195
with time's length bent to double measure
by delay crumbled the flower and pride
of Argos. Then against the bitter wind
the seer's voice clashed out
another medicine   200
more hateful yet, and spoke of Artemis, so that the kings
dashed their staves to the ground and could not hold their tears.

ANTISTROPHE D

The elder lord spoke aloud before them: 205
"My fate is angry if I disobey these,
but angry if I slaughter
this child, the beauty of my house,
with maiden bloodshed staining
these father's hands beside the altar.   210
What of these things goes now without disaster?
How shall I fail my ships

and lose my faith of battle?
To urge the wind-changing sacrifice of maiden's blood   215
angrily, for the wrath is great—it is right.° May all be well yet."

But when he put on necessity's yoke
he changed, and from the heart the breath came bitter
and sacrilegious, utterly infidel,   220
to warp a will now to be stopped at nothing.
The sickening in men's minds, mad,
reckless in first cruelty brings daring. He endured then
to sacrifice his daughter
in support of war waged for a woman,   225
first offering for the ships' sake.

Her supplications and her cries of father
were nothing, nor the child's lamentation
to kings passioned for battle.   230
The father prayed, called to his men to lift her
with strength of hand swept in her robes aloft
and prone above the altar, as you might lift
a goat for sacrifice—with a guard
against the lips' sweet edge, to check   235
the curse cried on the house of Atreus
by force and a bit's speechless power.

Pouring then to the ground her saffron mantle
she struck the sacrificers with   240
the eyes' arrows of pity,
lovely as in a painted scene, and striving
to speak—as many times
at the kind festive table of her father
she had sung, and in the clear voice of a stainless maiden   245
with love had graced the song
of worship when the third cup was poured.

ANTISTROPHE F

What happened next I saw not, neither speak it.
The crafts of Calchas fail not of outcome.
Justice tilts her scale so that those only 250
learn who suffer; and the future
you shall know when it has come; before then, forget it.
It is grief too soon given.
All will come clear in the next dawn's sunlight.
Let good fortune follow these things as 255
the one who is here desires,
our Apian land's single-hearted protector.°

(Enter Clytaemestra.)

CHORUS LEADER

I have come in reverence, Clytaemestra, of your power.
For when the man is gone and the throne void, his right
falls to the prince's lady, and honor must be given. 260
Is it some grace—or otherwise—that you have heard
to make you sacrifice at messages of good hope?
I should be glad to hear, but must not blame your silence.

CLYTAEMESTRA

As it was said of old, may the dawn child be born
to be an angel of blessing from the kindly night. 265
You shall know joy beyond all you ever hoped to hear.
The men of Argos have taken Priam's citadel.

CHORUS LEADER

What have you said? Your words escaped my doubting mind.

CLYTAEMESTRA

The Achaeans are in Troy. Is that not clear enough?

CHORUS LEADER

This slow delight steals over me to bring forth tears. 270

CLYTAEMESTRA

Yes, for your eyes betray the loyal heart within.

CHORUS LEADER

Yet how can I be certain? Is there some evidence?

CLYTAEMESTRA

There is, there must be; unless a god has lied to me.

CHORUS LEADER

Is it dream visions, easy to believe, you credit?

CLYTAEMESTRA

I accept nothing from a brain that is dull with sleep.   275

CHORUS LEADER

The charm, then, of some rumor, that made rich your hope?

CLYTAEMESTRA

Am I some young girl, that you find my thoughts so silly?

CHORUS LEADER

How long, then, is it since the citadel was stormed?

CLYTAEMESTRA

It was the night, the mother of this dawn I hailed.

CHORUS LEADER

What kind of messenger could come in speed like this?   280

CLYTAEMESTRA

Hephaestus, who cast forth the shining blaze from Ida.
And beacon after beacon picking up the flare
carried it here; Ida to the Hermaean horn
of Lemnos, where it shone above the isle, and next
the sheer rock face of Zeus on Athos caught it up;   285
and plunging skyward to arch the shoulders of the sea
the strength of the running flare in exultation,°
pine timbers flaming into gold, like the sunrise,
brought the bright message to Macistus' sentinel cliffs,
who, never slow nor in the carelessness of sleep   290
caught up, sent on his relay in the courier chain,
and far across Euripus' streams the beacon flare

carried to signal watchmen on Messapion.
These took it again in turn, and heaping high a pile
of silvery brush flamed it to throw the message on.   295
And the flare sickened never, but grown stronger yet
outleapt the river valley of Asopus like
the very moon for shining, to Cithaeron's scaur
to waken the next station of the flaming post.
These watchers, not contemptuous of the far-thrown blaze,   300
kindled another beacon vaster than commanded.
The light leaned high above Gorgopis' staring marsh,
and striking Aegyplanctus' mountaintop, drove on
yet one more relay, lest the flare die down in speed.
Kindled once more with stintless heaping force, they send   305
the beard of flame to hugeness, passing far beyond
the promontory that gazes on the Saronic strait
and flaming far, until it plunged at last to strike
the steep rock of Arachnus near at hand, our watchtower.
And thence there fell upon this house of Atreus' sons   310
the flare whose fathers mount to the Idaean beacon.
These are the changes on my torchlight messengers,
one from another running out the laps assigned.
The first and the last sprinters have the victory.
By such proof and such symbol I announce to you   315
my lord at Troy has sent his messengers to me.

CHORUS LEADER

The gods, lady, shall have my prayers and thanks straightway.
And yet to hear your story till all wonder fades
would be my wish, could you but tell it once again.

CLYTAEMESTRA

The Achaeans have got Troy, upon this very day.   320
I think the city echoes with a clash of cries.
Pour vinegar and oil into the selfsame bowl,
you could not say they mix in friendship, but fight on.
Thus variant sound the voices of the conquerors
and conquered, from the opposition of their fates.   325

Trojans are stooping now to gather in their arms
their dead, husbands and brothers; children lean to clasp
the aged who begot them, crying upon the death
of those most dear, from lips that never will be free.
The Achaeans have their midnight work after the fighting   330
that sets them down to feed on all the city has,
ravenous, headlong, by no rank and file assigned,
but as each man has drawn his shaken lot by chance.
And in the Trojan houses that their spears have taken
they settle now, free of the open sky, the frosts   335
and dampness of the evening; without sentinels set
they sleep the sleep of happiness the whole night through.
And if they reverence the gods who hold the city
and all the holy temples of the captured land,
they, the despoilers, might not be despoiled in turn.   340
Let not their passion overwhelm them; let no lust
seize on these men to violate what they must not.
The run to safety and home is yet to make; they must turn
the post, and run the backstretch of the double course.
Yet, though the host come home without offence to high   345
gods, even so the anger of these slaughtered men
may never sleep. Oh, let there be no fresh wrong done!
Such are the thoughts you hear from me, a woman merely.
Yet may the best win through, that none may fail to see.
Of all good things to wish this is my dearest choice.   350

CHORUS LEADER
My lady, you speak graciously like a prudent man.
I have listened to the proofs of your tale, and I believe,
and go to make my glad thanksgivings to the gods.
This pleasure is not unworthy of the grief that gave it.

                              (*Exit Clytaemestra into the palace.*)

[*chanting*]
O Zeus our lord and Night beloved,   355
bestower of power and beauty,

you slung above the bastions of Troy
the binding net, that none, neither great
nor young, might outleap
the gigantic toils   360
of enslavement and final disaster.
I gaze in awe on Zeus of the guests
who wrung from Alexander such payment.
He bent the bow with slow care, that neither
the shaft might hurdle the stars, nor fall   365
spent to the earth, short driven.

[singing]

STROPHE A

They have the stroke of Zeus to tell of.
This thing is clear and you may trace it.
He acted as he had decreed. A man thought
the gods deigned not to punish mortals   370
who trampled down the delicacy of things
inviolable. That man was wicked.
The curse on great daring
shines clear; it wrings atonement   375
from those high hearts that drive to evil,
from houses blossoming to pride
and peril. Let there be
wealth without tears; enough for
the wise man who will ask no further.   380
There is not any armor
in riches against perdition
for him who kicks the high altar
of Justice down to the darkness.

ANTISTROPHE A

Persuasion the persistent overwhelms him,   385
she, strong daughter of designing Ruin.
And every medicine is vain; the sin
smolders not, but burns to evil beauty.
As worthless bronze rubbed   390

at the touchstone relapses
to blackness and grime, so this man
tested shows vain
as a child that strives to catch the bird flying
and wins shame that shall bring down his city.   395
No god will hear such a man's entreaty,
but whoever turns to these ways
they strike him down in his wickedness.
This was Paris: he came
to the house of the sons of Atreus,   400
stole the woman away, and shamed
the guest's right of the board shared.

STROPHE B

She left among her people the stir and clamor
of shields and of spearheads,   405
the ships to sail and the armor.
She took to Ilium her dowry, death.
She stepped forth lightly between the gates
daring beyond all daring. And the prophets
about the great house wept aloud and spoke:
"Alas, alas for the house and for the champions,   410
alas for the bed signed with their love together.
Here now is silence, scorned, unreproachful.
The agony of his loss is clear before us.
Longing for her who lies beyond the sea
he shall see a phantom queen in his household.   415
Her images in their beauty
are bitterness to her lord now
where in the emptiness of eyes
all passion has faded."

ANTISTROPHE B

Shining in dreams the sorrowful   420
memories pass; they bring him
vain delight only.
It is vain, to dream and to see splendors,

and the image slipping from the arms' embrace
escapes, not to return again,   425
on wings drifting down the ways of sleep.
Such have the sorrows been in the house by the hearthside;
such have there been, and yet there are worse than these.
In all Hellas, for those who swarmed to the war,
the heartbreaking misery   430
shows in the house of each.
Many are they who are touched at the heart by these things.
Those they sent forth they knew;
now, in place of the young men
urns and ashes are carried home   435
to the houses of the fighters.

STROPHE C

The god of war, money changer of dead bodies,
held the balance of his spear in the fighting,
and from the corpse-fires at Ilium   440
sent to their dearest the dust
heavy and bitter with tears shed
packing smooth the urns with
ashes that once were men.
They praise them through their tears, how this man   445
knew well the craft of battle, how another
went down splendid in the slaughter:
and all for someone else's woman.
Thus they mutter in secrecy,
and the slow anger creeps below their grief   450
at Atreus' sons and their quarrels.
There by the walls of Ilium
the young men in their beauty keep
graves deep in the alien soil
they hated and they conquered.   455

ANTISTROPHE C

The citizens speak: their voice is deep with hatred.
The curse of the people must be paid for.

There lurks for me in the hooded night
terror of what may be told me.   460
The gods fail not to note
those who have killed many.
The black Furies, stalking the man
fortunate but without justice,
wrench back again the set of his life   465
and drop him to darkness. There among
the ciphers there is no more comfort
in power. And the vaunt of high glory
is bitterness; for god's thunderbolts
crash on the towering houses.°   470
Let me attain no envied wealth;
let me not plunder cities,
neither be captured in turn, and face
life in the power of another.

EPODE

From the beacon's bright message   475
the swift rumor runs
through the city. If this be real
who knows? Perhaps the gods have sent some lie to us.
    —Who of us is so childish or so short of wit
that by the beacon's messages   480
his heart flamed must sink down again
when the tale changes in the end?
    —It is like a woman indeed
to take the rapture before the fact has shown for true.
    Women believe too easily, are too quick to shift   485
from ground to ground; and swift indeed
the rumor voiced by a woman dies again.

CHORUS LEADER
    Now we° shall understand these torches and their shining,
    the beacons, and the interchange of flame and flame.   490
    They may be real; yet bright and dreamwise ecstasy
    in light's appearance might have charmed our hearts awry.

I see a herald coming from the beach, his brows
shaded with sprigs of olive; and upon his feet
the dust, dry sister of the mud, makes plain to me   495
that he will find a voice, not merely kindle flame
from mountain timber, and make signals from the smoke,
but tell us outright, whether to be happy, or—
but I shrink back from naming the alternative.
That which appeared was good; may yet more good be given.   500

And any man who prays that different things befall
the city, may he reap the crime of his own heart.

(Enter the Herald from the side.)

HERALD

Soil of my fathers, Argive earth I tread upon,
in daylight of the tenth year I have come back to you.
All my hopes broke but one, and this I have at last.   505
I never could have dared to dream that I might die
in Argos, and be buried in this beloved soil.
Hail to the Argive land and to its sunlight; hail
to its high sovereign, Zeus, and to the Pythian king.
May you no longer shower your arrows on our heads.   510
Beside Scamandrus you were grim; be satisfied
and turn to savior now and healer of our hurts,
my lord Apollo. Gods of the marketplace assembled,
I greet you all, and my own patron deity
Hermes, beloved herald, in whose right all heralds   515
are sacred; and you heroes that sent forth the host,
propitiously take back all that the spear has left.
O great hall of the kings and house beloved; seats
of sanctity; divinities that face the sun:
if ever before, look now with kind and glowing eyes   520
to greet our king in state after so long a time.
He comes, Lord Agamemnon, bearing light in gloom
to you, and to all that are assembled here.
Salute him with good favor, as he well deserves,
the man who has wrecked Ilium with the spade of Zeus   525

vindictive, whereby all their plain has been laid waste.
Gone are their altars; the sacred places of the gods
are gone, and scattered all the seed within the ground.
With such a yoke as this gripped to the neck of Troy
he comes, the king, Atreus' elder son, a man   530
fortunate to be honored far above all men
alive; not Paris nor the city tied to him
can boast he did more than was done him in return.
Guilty of rape and theft, condemned, he lost the prize
captured, and broke to sheer destruction all the house   535
of his fathers, with the very ground whereon it stood.
Twice over the sons of Priam have atoned their sins.

CHORUS LEADER
Hail and be glad, herald of the Achaean host.

HERALD
I am happy; I no longer ask the gods for death.

CHORUS LEADER
Did passion for your country so strip bare your heart?   540

HERALD
So that the tears broke in my eyes, for happiness.

CHORUS LEADER
You were taken with that sickness, then, that brings delight.

HERALD
How? I cannot deal with such words until I understand.

CHORUS LEADER
Struck with desire of those who loved as much again.

HERALD
You mean our country longed for us, as we for home?   545

CHORUS LEADER
So that I sighed, out of the darkness of my heart.

HERALD
Whence came this black thought to afflict the mind with fear?

CHORUS LEADER

Long since it was my silence kept disaster off.

HERALD

But how? There were some you feared when the kings went
away?

CHORUS LEADER

So much that as you said now, even death were grace. 550

HERALD

Well: the end has been good. And in the length of time
part of our fortune you could say held favorable,
but part we cursed again. And who, except the gods,
can live time through forever without any pain?
Were I to tell you of the hard work done, the nights 555
exposed, the cramped sea-quarters, the foul beds—what part
of day's disposal did we not cry out loud?
Ashore, the horror stayed with us and grew. We lay
against the ramparts of our enemies, and from
the sky, and from the ground, the meadow dews came out 560
to soak our clothes and fill our hair with lice. And if
I were to tell of wintertime, when all birds died,
the snows of Ida past endurance she sent down,
or summer heat, when in the lazy noon the sea
fell level and asleep under a windless sky— 565
but why live such grief over again? That time is gone
for us, and gone for those who died. Never again
need they rise up, nor care again for anything.
Why must a live man count the numbers of the slain,
why grieve at fortune's wrath that fades to break once more? 570
I call a long farewell to all our unhappiness.
For us, survivors of the Argive armament,
the pleasure wins, pain casts no weight in the opposite scale.
And here, in this sun's shining, we can boast aloud,
whose fame has gone with wings across the land and sea:° 575
"Upon a time the Argive host took Troy, and on

the houses of the gods who live in Hellas nailed
the spoils, to be the glory of days long ago."
And they who hear such things shall call this city bless'd
and the leaders of the host; and high the grace of god   580
shall be exalted, that did this. You have the story.

CHORUS LEADER

I must give way; your story shows that I was wrong.
Old men are always young enough to learn, with profit.
But Clytaemestra and her house must hear, above
others, this news that makes luxurious my life.   585

(*Clytaemestra enters from the palace.*)

CLYTAEMESTRA

I raised my cry of joy, and it was long ago
when the first beacon flare of message came by night
to speak of capture and of Ilium's overthrow.
But there was one who laughed at me, who said: "You trust   590
in beacons so, and you believe that Troy has fallen?
How like a woman, for the heart to lift so light."
Men spoke like that; they thought I wandered in my wits;
yet I made sacrifice, and in the womanish strain
voice after voice caught up the cry along the city   595
to echo in the temples of the gods and bless
and still the fragrant flame that melts the sacrifice.

Why should you tell me then the whole long tale at large
when from my lord himself I shall hear all the story?
But now, how best to speed my preparation to   600
receive my honored lord come home again—what else
is light more sweet for woman to behold than this,
to spread the gates before her husband home from war
and saved by god's hand?—take this message to the king:
Come, and with speed, back to the city that longs for him,   605
and may he find a wife within his house as true
as on the day he left her, watchdog of the house
gentle to him alone, fierce to his enemies,

and such a woman in all her ways as this, who has
not broken the seal upon her in the length of days.   610
With no man else have I known delight, nor any shame
of evil speech, more than I know how to temper bronze.

HERALD

A vaunt like this, so loaded as it is with truth,
it well becomes a highborn lady to proclaim.

CHORUS LEADER

Thus has she spoken to you, and well you understand,   615
words that impress interpreters whose thought is clear.
But tell me, herald; I would learn of Menelaus,
that power beloved in this land. Has he survived
also, and come with you back to his home again?

HERALD

I know no way to lie and make my tale so fair   620
that friends could reap joy of it for any length of time.

CHORUS LEADER

Is there no means to speak us fair, and yet tell the truth?
It will not hide, when truth and good are torn asunder.

HERALD

He is gone out of the sight of the Achaean host,
vessel and man alike. I speak no falsehood there.   625

CHORUS LEADER

Was it when he had put out from Ilium in your sight,
or did a storm that struck you both whirl him away?

HERALD

How like a master bowman you have hit the mark
and in your speech cut a long sorrow to brief stature.

CHORUS LEADER

But then the rumor in the host that sailed beside,   630
was it that he had perished, or might yet be living?

HERALD

No man knows. There is none could tell us that for sure
except the Sun, from whom this earth has life and increase.

CHORUS LEADER

How did this storm, by wrath of the divinities,
strike on our multitude at sea? How did it end?   635

HERALD

It is not well to stain the blessing of this day
with speech of evil weight. Such gods are honored apart.
And when the messenger of a shaken host, sad faced,
brings to his city news it prayed never to hear,
this scores one wound upon the body of the people;   640
and that from many houses many men are slain
by the two-lashed whip dear to the war god's hand, this turns
disaster double-bladed, bloodily made two.
The messenger so freighted with a charge of tears
should make his song of triumph at the Furies' door.   645
But, carrying the fair message of our hopes' salvation,
come home to a glad city's hospitality,
how shall I mix my gracious news with foul, and tell
of the storm on the Achaeans by god's anger sent?
For they, of old the deepest enemies, sea and fire,   650
made a conspiracy and gave their hand in oath
to blast in ruin our unhappy Argive army.
At night the sea began to rise in waves of death.
Ship against ship the Thracian stormwind shattered us,
and gored and split, our vessels, swept in violence   655
of storm and whirlwind, beaten by the breaking rain,
drove on in darkness, spun by the wicked shepherd's hand.
But when the sun came up again to light the dawn,
we saw the Aegean Sea blossoming with dead men,
the men of Achaea, and the wreckage of their ships.   660
For us, and for our ship, some god, no man, by guile
or by entreaty's force prevailing, laid his hand

upon the helm and brought us through with hull unscarred.
Life-giving fortune deigned to take our ship in charge
that neither riding in deep water she took the surf   665
nor drove to shoal and break upon some rocky shore.
But then, delivered from death at sea, in the pale day,
incredulous of our own luck, we shepherded
in our sad thoughts the fresh disaster of the fleet
so pitifully torn and shaken by the storm.   670
Now of these others, if there are any left alive
they speak of us as men who perished, must they not?
Even as we, who fear that they are gone. But may
it all come well in the end. For Menelaus: be sure
if any of them come back that he will be the first.   675
If he is still where some sun's gleam can track him down,
alive and open-eyed, by blessed hand of god
who willed that not yet should his seed be utterly gone,
there is some hope that he will still come home again.
You have heard all; and be sure, you have heard the truth.   680

                        (*Exit the Herald to the side.*)

CHORUS [*singing*]

                        STROPHE A
Who is he that named you so
fatally in every way?
Could it be some mind unseen
in divination of your destiny
shaping to the lips that name   685
for the bride of spears and blood,
Helen, a hell on earth? All too truly
hell for ships, hell for men and cities,
from the bower's soft curtained   690
and secluded luxury she sailed then,
driven on the giant west wind,
and armored men in their thousands came,
huntsmen down the oar blade's fading footprint   695

to struggle in blood with those
who by the banks of Simoeis
beached their hulls where the leaves break.

And on Ilium in truth
in the likeness of the name   700
the sure purpose of the Wrath drove
marriage with death: for the guest board
shamed, and Zeus kindly to strangers,
the vengeance wrought on those men
who graced in too loud voice the bride-song   705
fallen to their lot to sing,
the kinsmen and the brothers.
And changing its song's measure
the ancient city of Priam   710
chants in high strain of lamentation,
calling Paris him of the fatal marriage;
for it endured its life's end
in desolation and tears
and the piteous blood of its people.   715

Once a man fostered in his house
a lion cub, from the mother's milk
torn, craving the breast given.
In the first steps of its young life,   720
mild, it played with children
and delighted the old.
Caught in the arm's cradle
they pampered it like a newborn child,
shining-eyed and broken to the hand   725
to stay the stress of its hunger.

But it grew with time, and the lion
in the blood strain came out; it repaid

thanks to those who had fostered it
in blood and death for the sheep flocks,   730
a grim feast forbidden.
The house reeked with blood run,
nor could its people beat down the bane,
the giant murderer's onslaught.
This thing they raised in their house was blessed   735
by god to be priest of destruction.

STROPHE C

And that which first came to the city of Ilium,
call it a dream of calm
and the wind dying,
the loveliness and luxury of much gold,   740
the melting shafts of the eyes' glances,
the blossom that breaks the heart with longing.
But she turned in midstep of her course to make
bitter the consummation,   745
whirling on Priam's people
to blight with her touch and nearness.
Zeus hospitable sent her,
a Vengeance to make brides weep.

ANTISTROPHE C

It was made long since, grown old now among men,   750
this saying: human wealth
grown to fullness of stature
breeds again nor dies without issue.
From high good fortune in the blood   755
blossoms the quenchless agony.
But far from others I hold my own
mind; only the act of evil
breeds others to follow,
young sins in its own likeness.   760
Houses clear in their right are given
children in all loveliness.

So Outrage aging is made ripe
in men's dark actions,
ripe with the young Outrage   765
late or soon, when the dawn of destiny
comes and birth is given
to the spirit none may fight nor beat down,
sinful Daring; and in those halls
the black-visaged Disasters stamped   770
in the likeness of their fathers.

ANTISTROPHE D

But Righteousness still shines out
in the smoke of mean houses.
Her blessing is on the just man.   775
From high halls starred with gold by reeking hands
she turns back
with eyes that glance away to the simple in heart,
spurning the strength of gold
stamped false with flattery.   780
And all things she steers to fulfillment.

(Enter Agamemnon from the side in a chariot,
with Cassandra beside him.)

CHORUS [chanting]

Behold, my king: sacker of Troy's citadel,
own issue of Atreus.
How shall I hail you? How give honor   785
not shooting too high nor yet bending short
of this moment's fitness?
For many among men are they who set high
the show of honor, yet violate justice.
If one is distressed, all others are ready   790
to grieve with him: yet the teeth of sorrow
come nowhere near to their heart's edge.
And in joy likewise they show joy's semblance,
and torture the face to the false smile.

Yet the good shepherd, who knows his flock,   795
the eyes of men cannot lie to him,
who with water of feigned
love seem to smile from the true heart.
But I: when you marshaled this armament
for Helen's sake, I will not hide it,   800
in ugly style you were written in my heart
for steering aslant the mind's course
to bring home by blood
sacrifice and dead men that wild spirit.°
But now, in love drawn up from the deep heart,   805
not skimmed at the edge, we hail you.
You have won; your labor is made gladness.
Ask everyone: you will learn in time
which of your citizens have been just
in the city's service, which were reckless.   810

AGAMEMNON

To Argos first, and to the gods within the land,
I must give due greeting; they have worked with me to bring
me home; they helped me in the vengeance I have wrought
on Priam's city. Not from the lips of men the gods
heard justice, but in one firm cast they laid their votes   815
within the urn of blood that Ilium must die
and all her people; while above the opposite vase
the hand hovered and there was hope, but no vote fell.
The storm clouds of their ruin live; the ash that dies
upon them gushes still in smoke their pride of wealth.   820
For all this we must thank the gods with grace of much
high praise and memory, we who fenced within our toils
of wrath the city; and, because one woman strayed,
the beast of Argos broke them, the fierce young within
the horse, the armored people who marked out their leap   825
against the setting of the Pleiades. A wild
and bloody lion swarmed above the towers of Troy
to glut its hunger lapping at the blood of kings.

This to the gods, a prelude strung to length of words.
But, for the thought you spoke, I heard and I remember   830
and stand beside you. For I say that it is true.
In few men is it part of nature to respect
a friend's prosperity without begrudging him,
as envy's wicked poison settling to the heart
piles up the pain in one sick with unhappiness,   835
who, staggered under sufferings that are all his own,
winces again to the vision of a neighbor's bliss.
And I can speak, for I have seen, I know it well,
this mirror of companionship, this shadow's ghost,
all those who seemed my friends in their sincerity.   840
Just one of them, Odysseus, he who sailed unwilling,
once yoked to me pulled all his weight, nor ever slacked.
Dead though he be or living, I can say it still.

Now in the business of the city and the gods
we must ordain full conclave of all citizens   845
and take our counsel. We shall see what element
is strong, and plan that it shall keep its virtue still.
But that which must be healed—we shall use medicine,
or burn, or amputate, with kind intention, take
all means at hand that might beat down corruption's pain.   850
So to the king's house and the home about the hearth
I take my way, with greeting to the gods within
who sent me forth, and who have brought me home once
    more.
My prize was conquest; may it never fail again.

CLYTAEMESTRA
Grave gentlemen of Argolis assembled here,   855
I take no shame to speak aloud before you all
the love I bear my husband. In the lapse of time
modesty fades; it is human.
                              What I tell you now
I learned not from another; this was my own sad life
all the long years this man was gone at Ilium.   860

It is evil and a thing of terror when a wife
sits in the house forlorn with no man by, and hears
rumors that like a fever die to break again,
and men come in with news of fear, and on their heels
another messenger, with worse news to cry aloud   865
here in this house. Had Agamemnon taken all
the wounds of which the tale was carried home to me,
he had been cut full of gashes like a fishing net.
If he had died each time that rumor told his death,
he must have been some triple-bodied Geryon   870
back from the dead with threefold cloak of earth upon
his body, and killed once for every shape assumed.
Because such tales broke out forever on my rest,
many a time they cut me down and freed my throat   875
from the noose overslung where I had caught it fast.
And therefore is your son, in whom my love and yours
are sealed and pledged, not here to stand with us today,
Orestes. It were right; yet do not be amazed.
Strophius of Phocis, comrade in arms and faithful friend   880
to you, is keeping him. He spoke to me of peril
on two counts; of your danger under Ilium,
and here, of revolution and the clamorous people
who might cast down the council—since it lies in men's
nature to trample on the fighter already down.   885
Such my excuse to you, and without subterfuge.

For me: the rippling springs that were my tears have dried
utterly up, nor left one drop within. I keep
the pain upon my eyes where late at night I wept
over the beacons long ago set for your sake,   890
untended left forever. In the midst of dreams
the whisper that a gnat's thin wings could winnow broke
my sleep apart. I thought I saw you suffer wounds
more than the time that slept with me could ever hold.

Now all my suffering is past; with griefless heart   895
I hail this man, the watchdog of the fold and hall;

the rope that keeps the ship afloat; the post to grip
groundward the towering roof; a father's single child;
land seen by sailors after all their hope was gone;
splendor of daybreak shining from the night of storm;   900
the running spring a parched wayfarer strays upon.
Oh, it is sweet to escape from all necessity!

Such is my greeting to him, that he well deserves.
Let none bear malice; for the harm that went before
I took, and it was great.
                            Now, my beloved one,   905
step from your chariot; yet let not your foot, my lord,
sacker of Ilium, touch the earth. My maidens there!
Why this delay? Your task has been appointed you,
to strew the ground before his feet with tapestries.
Let there spring up into the house he never hoped   910
to see, where Justice leads him in, a crimson path.

In all things else, my heart's unsleeping care shall act
with the gods' aid to set aright what fate ordained.

> *(Clytaemestra's handmaidens spread a red*
> *carpet between the chariot and the door.)*

AGAMEMNON

Daughter of Leda, you who kept my house for me,
there is one way your welcome matched my absence well.   915
You strained it to great length. Yet properly to praise
me thus belongs by right to other lips, not yours.
And all this—do not try in woman's ways to make
me delicate, nor, as if I were some Asian prince
bow down to earth and with wide mouth cry out to me,   920
nor cross my path with jealousy by strewing the ground
with robes. Such state befits the gods, and none beside.
I am a mortal, a man; I cannot trample upon
these tinted splendors without fear thrown in my path.
I tell you, as a man, not god, to reverence me.   925

Discordant is the murmur at such treading down
of lovely things; while god's most lordly gift to man
is decency of mind. Call that man only bless'd
who has in sweet tranquility brought his life to close.
If I could only act as such, my hope is good.   930

CLYTAEMESTRA
Yet tell me this one thing, and do not cross my will.

AGAMEMNON
My will is mine. I shall not make it soft for you.

CLYTAEMESTRA
Might you in fear have vowed to do such things for god?

AGAMEMNON
Only if the one who advised so knew the full purpose.°

CLYTAEMESTRA
If Priam had won as you have, what would he have done?   935

AGAMEMNON
I well believe he might have walked on tapestries.

CLYTAEMESTRA
Be not ashamed before the criticism of men.

AGAMEMNON
The people murmur, and their voice is great in strength.

CLYTAEMESTRA
Yet he who goes unenvied shall not be admired.

AGAMEMNON
Surely this lust for conflict is not womanlike?   940

CLYTAEMESTRA
Yet for the mighty even to give way is grace.

AGAMEMNON
Does such a victory as this mean so much to you?

CLYTAEMESTRA

Oh yield! The power is yours. Freely give way to me.

AGAMEMNON

Since you must have it—here, let someone with all speed
take off these sandals, slaves for my feet to tread upon.   945
And as I crush these garments stained from the rich sea
let no god's eyes of hatred strike me from afar.
Great the extravagance, and great the shame I feel
to spoil such treasure and such silver's worth of weaving.

So much for all this. Take this stranger girl within   950
now, and be kind. The conqueror who uses softly
his power is watched benevolently by god from afar,
and this slave's yoke is one no man will wear from choice.
Gift of the host to me, and flower exquisite
from all my many treasures, she attends me here.   955

Now since my will was bent to listen to you in this
my feet crush crimson as I pass within the hall.

CLYTAEMESTRA

The sea is there, and who shall drain its yield? It breeds
precious as silver, ever of itself renewed,
the purple ooze wherein our garments shall be dipped.   960
And by god's grace this house keeps full sufficiency
of all. Poverty is a thing beyond its thought.
I could have vowed to trample many splendors down
had such decree been ordained from the oracles
those days when all my study was to bring home your life.   965
For when the root lives yet the leaves will come again
to fence the house with shade against the Dog Star's heat,
and now you have come home to keep your hearth and
    house,
you bring with you the symbol of our winter's warmth;
and when Zeus ripens the green clusters into wine   970
there shall be coolness in the house upon those days
because the master ranges his own halls once more.

Zeus, Zeus accomplisher, accomplish these my prayers.
Let your mind bring these things to pass. It is your will.

(Agamemnon and Clytaemestra enter the palace.
Cassandra remains in the chariot.)

CHORUS [*singing*]

STROPHE A

Why must this persistent fear   975
beat its wings so ceaselessly
and so close against my mantic heart?
Why this strain unwanted, unrepaid, thus prophetic?
Nor can valor of good hope   980
seated near the chambered depth
of the spirit cast it out
as dreams of dark fancy; and yet time
has buried in the mounding sand
the sea cables since that day°   985
when against Ilium
the army and the ships put to sea.

ANTISTROPHE A

Yet I have seen with these eyes,
Agamemnon home again.
Still the spirit sings, drawing deep   990
from within this unlyric threnody of the Fury.
Hope is gone utterly;
the sweet strength is far away.
Surely this is not fantasy.   995
Surely it is real, this whirl of drifts
that spin the stricken heart.
Still I pray; may all this
expectation fade as vanity
into unfulfillment, and not be.   1000

STROPHE B

Yet it is true: the high strength of men
knows no content with limitation. Sickness

chambered beside it beats at the wall between.
Man's fate that sets a true   1005
course yet may strike upon
the blind and sudden reefs of disaster.°
But if before such time, fear
throw overboard some precious thing
of the cargo, with deliberate cast,   1010
not all the house, laboring
with weight of ruin, shall go down,
nor sink the hull deep within the sea.
And great and affluent the gift of Zeus
in yield of plowed acres year on year   1015
makes void again sick starvation.

ANTISTROPHE B

But when the black and mortal blood of man
has fallen to the ground before his feet, who then   1020
can sing spells to call it back again?
Did Zeus not warn us once
when he struck to impotence
Asclepius, who in truth charmed back the dead men?
Had the gods not so ordained   1025
that fate should stand against fate
to check any man's excess,
my heart now would have outrun speech
to break forth the water of its grief.
But this is so; I murmur deep in darkness   1030
sore at heart; my hope is gone now
ever again to unwind some crucial good
from the flames about my heart.

(Enter Clytaemestra from the palace.)

CLYTAEMESTRA

Cassandra, you may go within the house as well,   1035
since Zeus in no unkindness has ordained that you
must share our lustral water, stand with the great throng

of slaves that flock to the altar of our household god.
Step from this chariot, then, and do not be so proud.
And think—they say that long ago Alcmene's son   1040
was sold in bondage and endured the bread of slaves.
But if constraint of fact forces you to such fate,
be glad indeed for masters ancient in their wealth.
They who have reaped success beyond their dreams of hope
are savage above need and standard toward their slaves.   1045
From us you shall have all you have the right to ask.

CHORUS LEADER

What she has spoken is for you, and clear enough.
Fenced in these fatal nets wherein you find yourself
you should obey her if you can; perhaps you cannot.

CLYTAEMESTRA

Unless she uses speech incomprehensible,   1050
barbarian, wild as the swallow's song, I speak
within her understanding, and she must obey.

CHORUS LEADER

Go with her. What she bids is best in circumstance
that binds you now. Obey, and leave this chariot seat.

CLYTAEMESTRA

I have no leisure to stand outside the house and waste   1055
time on this woman. At the central altarstone
the flocks are standing, ready for the sacrifice
we make to this glad day we never hoped to see.
You: if you are obeying my commands at all, be quick.
But if in ignorance you fail to comprehend,   1060
speak not, but make with your barbarian hand some sign.

CHORUS LEADER

I think this stranger girl needs some interpreter
who understands. She is like some captive animal.

CLYTAEMESTRA

No, she is in the passion of her own wild thoughts.

Leaving her captured city she has come to us   1065
untrained to take the curb, and will not understand
until her rage and strength have foamed away in blood.
I shall throw down no more commands for her contempt.

(Exit Clytaemestra into the palace.)

CHORUS LEADER
I, though, shall not be angry, for I pity her.
Come down, poor creature, leave the empty car. Give way   1070
to compulsion and take up the yoke that shall be yours.

(Cassandra steps down from the chariot.)

CASSANDRA [*singing throughout the following interchange, while the
Chorus Leader speaks in response*]
Oh shame upon the earth!
Apollo, Apollo!

CHORUS LEADER
You cry on Loxias in agony? He is not
the one who usually has to do with grief.   1075

CASSANDRA
Oh shame upon the earth!
Apollo, Apollo!

CHORUS LEADER
Now once again in bitter voice she calls upon
this god, who has not part in any lamentation.

CASSANDRA
Apollo, Apollo!   1080
Lord of the ways, my ruin.
You have undone me once again, and utterly.

CHORUS LEADER
I think she will be prophetic of her own disaster.
Even in the slave's heart the gift divine lives on.

CASSANDRA
Apollo, Apollo!   1085

Lord of the ways, my ruin.
Where have you led me now at last? What house is this?

CHORUS LEADER

The house of the Atreidae. If you understand
not that, I can tell you; and so much at least is true.

CASSANDRA

No, but a house that god hates, guilty within   1090
of kindred blood shed, torture of its own,°
the shambles for men's butchery, the dripping floor.

CHORUS LEADER

The stranger is keen-scented like some hound upon
the trail of blood that leads her to discovered death.

CASSANDRA

Behold there the witnesses to my faith.   1095
The small children wail for their own death
and the flesh roasted that their father fed upon.

CHORUS LEADER

We had been told before of this prophetic fame
of yours: we want no prophets in this place at all.

CASSANDRA

Ah, for shame, what can she purpose now?   1100
What is this new and huge
stroke of atrocity she plans within the house
to beat down the beloved beyond hope of healing?
Rescue is far away.

CHORUS LEADER

I can make nothing of these prophecies. The rest   1105
I understood; the city is full of the sound of them.

CASSANDRA

So cruel then, that you can do this thing?
The husband of your own bed
to bathe bright with water—how shall I speak the end?

This thing shall be done with speed. The hand gropes now, and the
     other   1110
hand follows in turn.

CHORUS LEADER

No, I am lost. After the darkness of her speech
I go bewildered in a mist of prophecies.

CASSANDRA

No, no, see there! What is that thing that shows?
Is it some net of death?   1115
Or is the trap the woman there, the murderess?
Let now the slakeless fury in the race
rear up to howl aloud over this monstrous death.

CHORUS LEADER

Upon what demon in the house do you call, to raise
the cry of triumph? All your speech makes dark my hope.   1120

CHORUS [*singing now and throughout the following interchange with*
Cassandra, who continues to sing as well]
And to the heart below trickles the pale drop
as in the hour of death
timed to our sunset and the mortal radiance.
Ruin is near, and swift.

CASSANDRA

See there, see there! Keep from his mate the bull.   1125
Caught in the folded web's
entanglement she pinions him and with the black horn
strikes. And he crumples in the watered bath.
Guile, I tell you, and death there in the caldron wrought.

CHORUS LEADER

I am not proud in skill to guess at prophecies,   1130
yet even I can see the evil in this thing.

CHORUS

From divination what good ever has come to men?
Art, and multiplication of words

drifting through tangled evil bring
terror to them that hear. 1135

CASSANDRA

Alas, alas for the wretchedness of my ill-starred life.
This pain flooding the song of sorrow is mine alone.
Why have you brought me here in all unhappiness?
Why, why? Except to die with him? What else could be?

CHORUS

You are possessed of god, inspired at heart 1140
to sing your own death
song, the wild lyric as
in clamor for Itys, Itys over and over again
her long life of tears weeping forever grieves
the brown nightingale. 1145

CASSANDRA

Oh for the nightingale's pure song and a fate like hers.
With fashion of beating wings the gods clothed her about
and a sweet life they gave her and without lamentation.
But mine is the sheer edge of the tearing iron.

CHORUS

Whence come, beat upon beat, driven of god, 1150
vain passions of tears?
Whence your cries, terrified, clashing in horror,
in wrought melody and the singing speech?
Whence take you the marks to this path of prophecy
and speech of terror? 1155

CASSANDRA

Oh marriage of Paris, death to the men beloved!
Alas, Scamandrus, water my fathers drank.
There was a time I too at your springs
drank and grew strong. Ah me,
for now beside the deadly rivers, Cocytus 1160
and Acheron, I must cry out my prophecies.

CHORUS

What is this word, too clear, you have uttered now?
A child could understand.
And deep within goes the stroke of the dripping fang
as mortal pain at the trebled song of your agony   1165
shivers the heart to hear.

CASSANDRA

O sorrow, sorrow of my city dragged to uttermost death.
O sacrifices my father made at the wall.
Flocks of the pastured sheep slaughtered there.
And no use at all   1170
to save our city from its pain inflicted now.
And I too, with brain ablaze in fever, shall go down.

CHORUS

This follows the run of your song.
Is it, in cruel force of weight,
some divinity kneeling upon you brings   1175
the death song of your passionate suffering?
I cannot see the end.

CASSANDRA [now speaking]

No longer shall my prophecies like some young girl
new-married glance from under veils, but bright and strong
as winds blow into morning and the sun's uprise   1180
shall wax along the swell like some great wave, to burst
at last upon the shining of this agony.
Now I will tell you plainly and from no cryptic speech;
bear me then witness, running at my heels upon
the scent of these old brutal things done long ago.   1185
There is a choir that sings as one, that shall not again
leave this house ever; the song thereof breaks harsh with
    menace.
And drugged to double fury on the wine of men's
blood shed, there lurks forever here a drunken rout
of ingrown vengeful spirits never to be cast forth.   1190

Hanging above the hall they chant their song of hate
and the old sin, and taking up the strain in turn
spit curses on that man who spoiled his brother's bed.
Did I go wide, or hit, like a real archer? Am I
some swindling seer who hawks his lies from door to door?   1195
Upon your oath, bear witness that I know by heart
the legend of ancient wickedness within this house.

CHORUS LEADER [*speaking*]
　And how could an oath, though cast in rigid honesty,
　do any good? And still we stand amazed at you,
　reared in an alien city far beyond the sea;   1200
　how can you strike, as if you had been there, the truth?

CASSANDRA
　Apollo was the seer who set me to this work.

CHORUS LEADER
　Struck with some passion for you, and himself a god?

CASSANDRA
　There was a time I blushed to speak about these things.

CHORUS LEADER
　True; they who prosper take on airs more delicate.   1205

CASSANDRA
　Yes, then; he wrestled with me, and he breathed delight.

CHORUS LEADER
　Did you come to the getting of children then, the two of you?

CASSANDRA
　I promised that to Loxias, but I broke my word.

CHORUS LEADER
　Were you already possessed with the skills of god?

CASSANDRA
　Yes; even then I read my city's destinies.   1210

CHORUS LEADER

So Loxias' wrath did you no harm? How could that be?

CASSANDRA

For this my trespass, none believed me ever again.

CHORUS LEADER

But we do; all that you foretell seems true to us.

CASSANDRA

But this is evil, see!
Now once again the pain of grim, true prophecy   1215
shivers my whirling brain in a storm of things foreseen.
Look there, see what is hovering above the house,
so small and young, imaged as in the shadow of dreams,
like children almost, killed by those most dear to them,
and their hands filled with their own flesh, as food to eat.   1220
I see them holding out the inward parts, the vitals,
oh pitiful, that meat their father tasted of . . .
I tell you: There is one that plots vengeance for this,
the strengthless lion rolling in his master's bed,
who keeps, ah me, the house against his lord's return;   1225
my lord too, now that I wear the slave's yoke on my neck.
King of the ships, who tore up Ilium by the roots,
what does he know of this accursed bitch, who licks
his hand, who fawns on him with lifted ears, who like
a secret death shall strike the coward's stroke, nor fail?   1230
No, this is daring when the female shall strike down
the male. What can I call her and be right? What beast
of loathing? Viper double-fanged, or Scylla witch
holed in the rocks and bane of men that range the sea;
smoldering mother of death to breathe relentless hate   1235
on those most dear. How she stood up and howled aloud
and unashamed, as at the breaking point of battle,
in feigned gladness for his salvation from the sea!
What does it matter now if men believe or no?
What is to come will come. And soon you too will stand   1240
beside, to murmur in pity that my words were true.

CHORUS LEADER

Thyestes' feast upon the flesh of his own children
I understand in terror at the thought, and fear
is on me hearing truth and no tale fabricated.
The rest: I heard it, but wander still far from the course.   1245

CASSANDRA

I tell you, you shall look on Agamemnon dead.

CHORUS LEADER

Peace, peace, poor woman; put those bitter lips to sleep.

CASSANDRA

Useless; there is no god of healing in this story.

CHORUS LEADER

Not if it must be; may it somehow fail to come.

CASSANDRA

You pray, yes; but they—they plan to strike, and kill.   1250

CHORUS LEADER

What man is it who moves this beastly thing to be?

CASSANDRA

What man? You did mistake my divination then.

CHORUS LEADER

It may be; I could not follow through the schemer's plan.

CASSANDRA

Yet I know Greek; I think I know it far too well.

CHORUS LEADER

And Pythian oracles are Greek, yet hard to read.   1255

CASSANDRA

Oh, flame and pain that sweeps me once again! My lord,
Apollo, King of Light, the pain, aye me, the pain!
This is the woman-lioness, who goes to bed
with the wolf, when her proud lion ranges far away,

and she will cut me down; as a wife mixing drugs   1260
she wills to shred the virtue of my punishment
into her bowl of wrath as she makes sharp the blade
against her man, death that he brought a mistress home.
Why do I wear these mockeries upon my body,
this staff of prophecy, these garlands at my throat?   1265
At least I will spoil you before I die. Out, down,
break, damn you! This for all that you have done to me.
Make someone else, not me, luxurious in disaster . . .
Lo now, this is Apollo who has stripped me here
of my prophetic robes. He watched me all the time   1270
wearing this glory, mocked by all, my dearest ones
who hated me with all their hearts, so vain, so wrong;
called like some gypsy wandering from door to door
beggar, corrupt, half-starved, and I endured it all.
And now the seer has done with me, his prophetess,   1275
and led me into such a place as this, to die.
Lost are my father's altars, but the block is here
to reek with sacrificial blood, my own. We two
must die, yet die not vengeless by the gods. For there
shall come one to avenge us also, born to slay   1280
his mother, and to wreak death for his father's blood.
Outlaw and wanderer, driven far from his own land,
he will come back to cope these stones of inward hate.
For this is a strong oath and sworn by the high gods,°
that he shall cast them headlong for his father felled.   1285
Why am I then so pitiful? Why must I weep?
Since once I saw the citadel of Ilium
die as it died, and those who broke the city, doomed
by the gods, fare as they have fared accordingly,
I will go through with it. I too will take my fate.   1290
I call as on the gates of death upon these gates
to pray only for this thing, that the stroke be true,
and that with no convulsion, with a rush of blood
in painless death, I may close up these eyes, and rest.

CHORUS LEADER

O woman much enduring and so greatly wise,   1295
you have said much. But if this thing you know be true,
this death that comes upon you, how can you, serene,
walk to the altar like a driven ox of god?

CASSANDRA

Friends, there is no escape for any longer time.

CHORUS LEADER

Yet the last bit of time is to be honored most.   1300

CASSANDRA

The day is here and now; I cannot win by flight.

CHORUS LEADER

Woman, be sure your heart is brave; you can endure much.

CASSANDRA

None but the most unhappy ever hear such praise.

CHORUS LEADER

Yet there is a grace on mortals who so nobly die.

CASSANDRA

Alas for you, father, and for your lordly sons.   1305
Ah!

CHORUS LEADER

What now? What terror whirls you backward from the door?

CASSANDRA

Foul, foul!

CHORUS LEADER

What foulness then, unless some horror in the mind?

CASSANDRA

That room within reeks with blood like a slaughterhouse.

CHORUS LEADER

What then? Only these animals butchered at the hearth.   1310

CASSANDRA

There is a breath about it like an open grave.

CHORUS LEADER

This is no Syrian pride of frankincense you mean.

CASSANDRA

So. I am going in, and mourning as I go
my death and Agamemnon's. Let my life be done.
Ah friends,   1315
truly this is no wild bird fluttering at a bush,
nor vain my speech. Bear witness to me when I die,
when falls for me, a woman slain, another woman,
and when a man dies for this wickedly mated man.
Here in my death I claim this stranger's grace of you.   1320

CHORUS LEADER

Poor wretch, I pity you the fate you see so clear.

CASSANDRA

Yet once more will I speak, and not this time my own
death's threnody. I call upon the Sun in prayer
against that ultimate shining when the avengers strike
these monsters down in blood, that they avenge as well   1325
one simple slave who died, a small thing, lightly killed.
Alas, poor men, their destiny. When all goes well
a shadow will overthrow it. If it be unkind
one stroke of a wet sponge wipes all the picture out;
and that is far the most unhappy thing of all.   1330

                        (*Exit Cassandra into the palace.*)

CHORUS [*chanting*]

High fortune is a thing insatiable
for mortals. There is no man who shall point
his finger to drive it back from the door
and speak the words: "Come no longer."
Now to this man the blessed ones have given   1335
Priam's city to be captured

and return in the gods' honor.
Must he give blood for generations gone,
die for those slain and in death pile up
more death to come for the blood shed?   1340
What mortal else who hears shall claim
he was born immune to the demon of harm?

AGAMEMNON   *(Inside the house.)*
  Ah, I am struck a deadly blow and deep within!

CHORUS LEADER
  Silence: who cried out that he was stabbed to death within
    the house?

AGAMEMNON
  Ah me, again, they struck again. I am wounded twice.   1345

CHORUS LEADER
  How the king cried out aloud to us! I believe the thing is
    done.
  Come, let us put our heads together, try to find some safe way
    out.

CHORUS   *(Each member speaking excitedly in turn.)*
  Listen, let me tell you what I think is best to do.
  Let the herald call all citizens to rally here.

  No, better to burst in upon them now, at once,   1350
  and take them with the blood still running from their blades.

  I am with this man and I cast my vote to him.
  Act now. This is the perilous and instant time.

  Anyone can see it, by these first steps they have taken,
  they purpose to be tyrants here upon our city.   1355

  Yes, for we waste time, while they trample to the ground
  deliberation's honor, and their hands sleep not.

  I cannot tell which counsel of yours to call my own.
  It is the man of action who can plan as well.°

I feel as he does; nor can I see how by words   1360
we shall set the dead man back upon his feet again.

Do you mean, to drag our lives out long, that we must yield
to those shaming the house, and leadership of such as these?

No, we can never endure that; better to be killed.
Death is a softer thing by far than tyranny.   1365

Shall we, by no more proof than that he cried in pain,
be sure, as by divination, that our lord is dead?

Yes, we should know what is true before we speak our mind.
Here is sheer guessing and far different from sure
     knowledge.

From all sides the voices multiply to make me choose   1370
this course; to learn first how it stands with Agamemnon.

> (*The doors of the palace open, disclosing the bodies of Agamemnon
> and Cassandra, with Clytaemestra standing over them.*)

CLYTAEMESTRA
Much have I said before to serve necessity,
but I will feel no shame now to unsay it all.
How else could I, arming hate against hateful men
disguised in seeming tenderness, fence high the nets   1375
of ruin beyond overleaping? Thus to me
the conflict born of ancient bitterness is not
a thing new thought upon, but pondered deep in time.
I stand now where I struck him down. The thing is done.
Thus have I wrought, and I will not deny it now.   1380
That he might not escape nor beat aside his death,
as fishermen cast their huge circling nets, I spread
deadly abundance of rich robes, and caught him fast.
I struck him twice. In two great cries of agony
he buckled at the knees and fell. When he was down   1385
I struck him the third blow, in thanks and reverence
to Zeus beneath the ground, the prayed-for Savior of the dead.
Thus he went down, and the life struggled out of him;

and as he died he spattered me with the dark red
and violent driven rain of bitter-savored blood   1390
to make me glad, as plants stand strong amidst the showers
of god in glory at the birthtime of the buds.

These being the facts, elders of Argos assembled here,
be glad, if it be your pleasure; but for me, I glory.
If libations were proper to pour above the slain,   1395
this man deserved, more than deserved, such sacrament.
He filled our cup with evil things unspeakable
and now himself come home has drunk it to the dregs.

CHORUS LEADER
    We stand here stunned. How can you speak this way, with
        mouth
    so arrogant, to vaunt above your fallen lord?   1400

CLYTAEMESTRA
    You try me out as if I were a woman and vain;
    but my heart is not fluttered as I speak before you.
    You know it. You can praise or blame me as you wish;
    it is all one to me. That man is Agamemnon,
    my husband; he is dead; the work of this right hand   1405
    that struck in strength of righteousness. And that is that.

CHORUS [singing]
                        STROPHE A
    Woman, what evil thing planted upon the earth
    or dragged from the running salt sea could you have tasted now
    to show such brutality and walk in the people's hate?
    You have cast away, you have cut away. You shall go homeless now,   1410
    crushed with men's bitterness.

CLYTAEMESTRA
    Now it is I you vote to be cast out from my city
    with men's hate heaped and curses roaring in my ears.
    Yet look upon this dead man; you did not cross him once
    when with no thought more than as if a beast were
        butchered,   1415

when his ranged pastures swarmed with the deep fleece of
    flocks,
he slaughtered at the altar his own child, my pain
grown into love, to charm away the winds of Thrace.
Were you not bound to hunt him then clear of this soil
for the guilt stained upon him? Yet you hear what I   1420
have done, and lo, you are a stern judge. But I say to you:
go on and threaten me, but know that I am ready,
if fairly you can beat me down beneath your hand,
for you to rule; but if the god grant otherwise,
you shall be taught—too late, for sure—to keep your place.   1425

CHORUS [*singing*]

ANTISTROPHE A

Big are your thoughts, your speech is a clamor of pride.
Swung to the red act drives the fury within your brain
signed clear in the flecks of blood on your eyes.
Yet to come is stroke given for stroke
avenging, when you are forlorn of friends.   1430

CLYTAEMESTRA

Now hear you this, the right behind my sacrament:
By my child's Justice driven to fulfillment, by
her Wrath and Fury, to whom I sacrificed this man,
the hope that walks my chambers is not traced with fear
while yet Aegisthus makes the fire shine in my hearth,   1435
my good friend, now as always, who shall be for us
the shield of our defiance, no weak thing; while he,
this other, is fallen, stained with this woman you behold,
plaything of all the golden girls at Ilium;
and here lies she, the captive of his spear, who saw   1440
wonders, who shared his bed, the wise in revelations
and loving mistress, who yet knew the feel as well
of the men's rowing benches. Their reward is not
unworthy. He lies there; and she who swanlike cried
aloud her lyric dying lamentation, now   1445

lies next to him, his lover, and to me has given
a delicate excitement, spicing my delight.°

CHORUS [*singing*]

STROPHE B

O that in speed, without pain
and the slow bed of sickness,
death could come to us now, death that forever   1450
carries sleep without ending, now that our lord is down,
our shield, kindest of men,
who for a woman's grace suffered so much,
struck down at last by a woman.

[*chanting*]
Alas, Helen, crazed heart   1455
for the multitudes, for the thousand lives
you killed under Troy's shadow:
now as your final memorial,
you're adorned in blood never to be washed out.   1460
Surely a demon then
of Strife walked in the house, men's agony.

CLYTAEMESTRA [*chanting throughout the following interchange*
with the Chorus]

No, be not so harsh, and don't invoke
in prayer death's ending,
neither turn all wrath against Helen
for men dead, that she alone killed   1465
all those Danaan lives, to work
the grief that is past all healing.

CHORUS [*singing*]

ANTISTROPHE B

Spirit that kneels on this house and on the two
strains of the blood of Tantalus,
in the hands and hearts of women you steer   1470
the strength tearing my heart.
Standing above the corpse, obscene

as some carrion crow it sings
the crippled song and is proud.°

CLYTAEMESTRA

Now have you set the speech of your lips   1475
straight, calling by name
the spirit thrice glutted that lives in this race.
From it, deep in the nerve is given
the love and the blood drunk, that before
the old wound dries, it bleeds again.   1480

CHORUS [singing]

STROPHE C

Surely it is a huge
and angry spirit haunting the house you cry;
alas, the bitter story
of a doom that shall never be done with;
and all through Zeus, Zeus,   1485
first cause, prime mover.
For what thing without Zeus is done among mortals?
What here is without god's blessing?

[chanting]
O king, my king,
how shall I weep for you?   1490
What can I say out of my heart of pity?
Caught in this spider's web you lie.
Your life gasped out in indecent death,
struck prone to this shameful bed
by your lady's hand of treachery   1495
and the stroke twin-edged of the iron.

CLYTAEMESTRA

Can you claim I have done this?
Speak of me never
more as the wife of Agamemnon.°
In the image of this corpse's queen   1500

the old stark avenger
of Atreus for his revel of hate
struck down this man,
last blood for the slaughtered children.

CHORUS [singing]

ANTISTROPHE C

What man shall testify   1505
your hands are clean of this murder?
How? How? Yet from his father's blood
might swarm some fiend to assist you.
The black ruin that shoulders
through the streaming blood of brothers   1510
strides at last where he shall win requital
for the children who were eaten.

[chanting]
O king, my king
how shall I weep for you?
What can I say out of my heart of pity?   1515
Caught in this spider's web you lie,
your life gasped out in indecent death,
struck prone to this shameful bed
by your lady's hand of treachery
and the stroke twin-edged of the iron.   1520

CLYTAEMESTRA
No shame, I think, in the death given
this man. And did he not
first of all in this house wreak death
by treachery?
The flower of this man's love and mine,   1525
Iphigeneia of the many tears—
he dealt with her even as he has suffered now.°
So let his speech in Death's house be not loud.
With the sword he struck;
with the sword he paid for his own act.

CHORUS [*singing*]

My thoughts are swept away and I go bewildered.   1530
Where shall I turn the brain's
activity in speed when the house is falling?
There is fear in the beat of the blood rain breaking
wall and tower. The drops come thicker.
Still fate grinds on yet more stones the blade   1535
for more acts of terror.

[*chanting*]
Earth, my earth, why did you not fold me under
before ever I saw this man lie dead
fenced in by the tub of silver?   1540
Who shall bury him? Who shall mourn him?
Shall you dare this who have killed
your lord? Make lamentation,
render the graceless grace to his soul
for huge things done in wickedness?   1545
Who over this great man's grave shall lay
the blessing of tears
worked soberly from a true heart?   1550

CLYTAEMESTRA

Not for you to speak of such tendance.
Through us he fell,
by us he died; we shall bury.
There will be no tears in this house for him.
It must be Iphigeneia   1555
his child—who else
shall greet her father by the whirling stream
and the ferry of tears
to close him in her arms and kiss him.

CHORUS [*singing*]

Here is anger for anger. Between them   1560
who shall judge lightly?

The spoiler is robbed; he killed, he has paid.
The truth stands ever beside god's throne
eternal: he who has done shall suffer; that is law.
Then who shall tear the curse from their blood?   1565
The house is glued to ruin.

CLYTAEMESTRA

You see truth in the future
at last. Yet I wish
to seal my oath with the Spirit
in the house: I will endure all things as they stand   1570
now, hard though it be. Hereafter
let it go forth to make bleed with death
and guilt the houses of others.
I will take some small
measure of our riches, and be content
that I swept from these halls   1575
the murder, the sin, and the fury.

(Enter Aegisthus from the side, with his armed bodyguard.)

AEGISTHUS

O splendor and triumph of this day of justice!
Now I can say once more that the high gods look down
on mortal crimes to vindicate the right at last,
now that I see this man—sweet sight—before me here   1580
sprawled in the tangling nets of fury, to atone
the calculated evil of his father's hand.
For Atreus, this man's father, King of Argolis—
I tell you the clear story—drove my father forth,
Thyestes, his own brother, who had challenged him   1585
in his king's right—forth from his city and his home.
Yet poor Thyestes came again to supplicate
the hearth, and win some grace. He found a safe portion
nor soiled the doorstone of his fathers with blood spilled.
Not his own blood. But Atreus, this man's godless sire,   1590
angrily hospitable set a feast for him,
in seeming a glad day of fresh meat slain and good

cheer; then served my father his own children's flesh
to feed on. For he carved away the extremities,
hands, feet, and cut the flesh apart, and covered them   1595
served in a dish to my father at his table apart,
who with no thought for the featureless meal before him ate
that ghastly food whose curse works now before your eyes.
But when he knew the terrible thing that he had done,
he spat the dead meat from him with a cry, recoiled   1600
and kicked the table over, pledging with strength his curse:
"Thus crash in ruin all the seed of Pleisthenes."
Out of such acts you see this dead man stricken here,
and it was I, in my right, who wrought this murder, I
third-born to my unhappy father, and with him   1605
driven, a helpless baby in arms, to banishment.
Yet I grew up, and justice brought me home again,
till from afar I laid my hands upon this man,
since it was I who pieced together the deadly plot.
Now I can die in honor again, if die I must,   1610
having seen him caught in the nets of his just punishment.

CHORUS LEADER

Aegisthus, this strong vaunting in distress is vile.
You claim that you deliberately killed the king,
you, and you only, planned the pity of this death.
I tell you then: There shall be no escape, your head   1615
shall face the stones of anger from the people's hands.

AEGISTHUS

So loud from you, stooped to the meanest rowing bench
with the ship's masters lordly on the deck above?
You are old men; well, you shall learn how hard it is,
at your age, to be taught how to behave yourselves.   1620
But there are chains, there is starvation with its pain,
excellent teachers of good manners to old men,
wise surgeons and exemplars. Look! Can you not see it?
Kick not at the goads for fear you hit them, and be hurt.

CHORUS LEADER

So then you, like a woman, waited the war out   1625
here in the house, shaming the master's bed with lust,
and planned against the lord of war this treacherous death?

AEGISTHUS

It is just such words as these will make you cry in pain.
Not yours the lips of Orpheus, no, quite otherwise—
his voice of rapture led all creatures in his train;   1630
you shall be led away, for babyish cries sobbed out
in rage. Once broken, you will be easier to deal with.

CHORUS LEADER

How shall you be lord of the men of Argos, you
who planned the murder of this man, yet could not dare
to act it out and cut him down with your own hand?   1635

AEGISTHUS

No, clearly the deception was the woman's part,
and I was suspect, that had hated him so long.
Still with his money I shall endeavor to control
the citizens. The mutinous man shall feel the yoke
drag at his neck, no oat-fed racehorse running free,   1640
but hunger, grim companion of the dark dungeon
shall see him trudging, broken to the hand at last.

CHORUS LEADER

But why, why then, you coward, could you not have slain
your man yourself? Why must it be his wife who killed,
to curse the country and the gods within the ground?   1645
Oh, can Orestes live, be somewhere in sunlight still?
Shall fate grown gracious ever bring him back again
in strength of hand to overwhelm these murderers?

AEGISTHUS

You shall learn then, since you stick to stubbornness of
    mouth and hand.

CHORUS LEADER°
Come on now, my trusty comrades: here is work for you
  to do.   1650

AEGISTHUS
Come on now! Let every man clap fist upon his ready sword.

CHORUS LEADER
I as well am ready-handed; I am not afraid of death.

AEGISTHUS
Death you said and death it shall be; so I take up the word of
  fate.

CLYTAEMESTRA
No, my dearest, dearest of all men, we have done enough. No
  more
violence. Here is a monstrous harvest and a bitter reaping
  time.   1655
There is pain enough already. Let us not be bloody now.
Honored gentlemen of Argos, go to your homes now and
  give way°
to the stress of fate and season. We could not do otherwise
than we did. If this is the end of suffering, we can be content
broken as we are by the brute heel of angry destiny.   1660
Thus a woman speaks among you. Shall men deign to
  understand?

AEGISTHUS
Yes, but think of these foolish lips that blossom° into leering
  gibes;
think of the taunts they spit against me daring destiny and
  power,
sober opinion lost in insults hurled against my majesty.

CHORUS LEADER
It was never the Argive way to grovel at a vile man's feet.   1665

AEGISTHUS
I shall not forget this; in the days to come I shall be there.

CHORUS LEADER

Nevermore, if god's guiding hand brings Orestes home again.

AEGISTHUS

Exiles feed on empty dreams of hope. I know it. I was one.

CHORUS LEADER

Have your way, gorge and grow fat, soil justice, while the
power is yours.

AEGISTHUS

You shall pay, make no mistake, for this foolishness.   1670

CHORUS LEADER

Crow and strut, brave cockerel by your hen; you have no
threats to fear.

CLYTAEMESTRA

Do not heed their empty yappings; come now, dearest, you
and I

have the power; we two shall bring good order to our house at
least.

(Exit Aegisthus and Clytaemestra into the palace.)

THE LIBATION BEARERS

Characters   ORESTES, son of Agamemnon and Clytaemestra
PYLADES, his friend
ELECTRA, his sister
CHORUS of Asian serving-women
A SERVANT (doorkeeper)
CLYTAEMESTRA, queen of Argos; now wife of
Aegisthus
THE NURSE, Cilissa
AEGISTHUS, now king of Argos
A FOLLOWER of Aegisthus

Scene: Argos, in front of the palace.

(Enter Orestes and Pylades, from the side.)

ORESTES
Hermes, lord of the dead, you who watch over the powers
of my fathers, be my savior and stand by my claim.°
Here is my own soil that I walk. I have come home;
and by this mounded gravebank I invoke my father
to hear, to listen.   5
He met his end in violence through a woman's treacherous
    tricks . . .
Here is a lock of hair for Inachus, who made
me grow to manhood. Here a strand to mark my grief.
I was not by, my father, to mourn for your death
nor stretched my hand out when they took your corpse away.

(Enter the Chorus, with Electra, from the other side.)

But what can this mean that I see, this group that comes   10
of women veiled in dignities of black? At what
sudden occurrence can I guess? Is this some new
wound struck into our house? I think they bring these urns
to pour, in my father's honor, to appease the powers
below. Can I be right? Surely, I think I see   15
Electra, my own sister, walk in bitter show
of mourning. Zeus, Zeus, grant me vengeance for my father's
murder. Stand and fight beside me, of your grace.
Pylades, stand we out of their way. So may I learn
the meaning of these women; what their prayer would ask.   20

(Orestes and Pylades conceal themselves, to one side.)

CHORUS [*singing*]

STROPHE A

I came in haste out of the house
to carry libations, hurt by the hard stroke of hands.
My cheek shows bright, ripped in the bloody furrows
of nails gashing the skin.   25
This is my life: to feed the heart on hard-drawn breath.
And in my grief, with splitting weft
of ragtorn linen across my heart's
brave show of robes
came sound of my hands' strokes   30
in sorrows whence smiles are fled.

ANTISTROPHE A

Terror, the dream diviner of
this house, belled clear, shuddered the skin, blew wrath
from sleep, a cry in night's obscure watches,
a voice of fear deep in the house,   35
dropping deadweight in women's inner chambers.
And they who read the dream meanings
and spoke under guarantee of god
told how under earth

dead men held a grudge still   40
and smoldered at their murderers.

On such grace without grace, evil's turning aside
(Earth, Earth, kind mother!)
bent, the godless woman   45
sends me forth. But terror
is on me for this word let fall.
What can wash off the blood once spilled upon the ground?
O hearth soaked in sorrow,
O wreckage of a fallen house.   50
Sunless and where men fear to walk
the mists huddle upon this house
where the high lords have perished.

The pride not to be warred with, fought with, not to be beaten down   55
of old, sounded in all men's
ears, in all hearts sounded,
has shrunk away. A man
goes in fear. High fortune,
this in man's eyes is god and more than god is this.   60
But, as a beam balances, so
sudden disasters wait, to strike
some in the brightness, some in gloom
of half dark in their elder time.
Desperate night holds others.   65

Through too much glut of blood drunk by our fostering ground
the vengeful gore is caked and hard, will not drain through.
The deep-run ruin carries away
the man of guilt. Swarming infection boils within.   70

For one who assaults the bride's pure bed, there is no cure.
All the world's waters running in a single drift

may try to wash blood from the hand
of the stained man; they only bring new blood guilt on.

But as for me: gods have forced on my city   75
resisted fate. From our fathers' houses
they led us here, to take the lot of slaves.
And mine it is to wrench my will, and consent
to their commands, right or wrong,
to beat down my edged hate.   80
And yet under veils I weep
the futile destinies of
my lord; and freeze with sorrow in the secret heart.

ELECTRA

Attendant women, who order our house, since you
are with me in this supplication and escort   85
me here, be also my advisors in this rite.
What shall I say, as I pour out these outpourings
of sorrow? How say the good word, how make my prayer
to my father? Shall I say I bring it to the man
beloved, from a loving wife, and mean my mother? I   90
have not the daring to say this, nor know what else
to say, as I pour this liquid on my father's tomb.°
Shall I say this sentence, regular in human use:
"Grant good return to those who send to you these flowers
of honor: gifts to match the—evil they have done."   95
Or, quiet and dishonored, as my father died
shall I pour out this offering for the ground to drink,
and go, like one who empties garbage out of doors,
and turn my eyes, and throw the vessel far away?
Dear friends, in this deliberation stay with me.   100
We hold a common hatred in this house. Do not
for fear of any, hide your thought inside your heart.
The day of destiny waits for the free man as well
as for the man enslaved beneath an alien hand.
If you know any better course than mine, tell me.   105

CHORUS LEADER

In reverence for your father's tomb as if it were
an altar, I will speak my heart's thought, as you ask.

ELECTRA

Tell me then, please, as you respect my father's grave.

CHORUS LEADER

Say words of grace for those of goodwill, as you pour.

ELECTRA

Whom of those closest to me can I call my friend?   110

CHORUS LEADER

Yourself first; all who hate Aegisthus after that.

ELECTRA

You mean these prayers shall be for you, and for myself?

CHORUS LEADER

You see it now; but it is you whose thought this is.

ELECTRA

Is there some other we should bring in on our side?

CHORUS LEADER

Remember Orestes, though he wanders far away.   115

ELECTRA

That was well spoken; you did well reminding me.

CHORUS LEADER

Remember, too, the murderers, and against them . . .

ELECTRA

What shall I say? Guide and instruct my ignorance.

CHORUS LEADER

Invoke the coming of some man, or more than man.

ELECTRA

To come to judge them, or to give them punishment?   120

CHORUS LEADER

　　Say simply: "one to kill them, for the life they took."

ELECTRA

　　I can ask this, and not be wrong in the gods' eyes?

CHORUS LEADER

　　Of course, to hurt your enemy when he struck first.

ELECTRA

　　Almighty herald of the world above, the world
　　below:° Hermes, lord of the dead, help me; announce
　　my prayers to the charmed spirits underground, who watch　　　125
　　over my father's house, that they may hear. Tell Earth
　　herself, who brings all things to birth, who gives them
　　　　strength,
　　then gathers their big yield into herself at last.
　　I myself pour these lustral waters to the dead,
　　and speak, and call upon my father: Pity me;　　　130
　　pity your own Orestes. How shall we be lords
　　in our house? We have been sold, and go as wanderers
　　because our mother bought herself, for us, a man,
　　Aegisthus, he who helped her hand to cut you down.
　　Now I am what a slave is, and Orestes lives　　　135
　　outcast from his great properties, while they go proud
　　in the high style and luxury of what you worked
　　to win. By some good fortune let Orestes come
　　back home. Such is my prayer, my father. Hear me; hear.
　　And for myself, grant that I be more temperate　　　140
　　of heart than my mother; that I act with purer hand.
　　Such are my prayers for us; but for our enemies,
　　father, I pray that your avenger come, that they
　　who killed you shall be killed in turn, as they deserve.
　　Between my prayer for good and prayer for good I set　　　145
　　this prayer for evil; and I speak it against Them.
　　For us, bring blessings up into the world. Let Earth
　　and conquering Justice, and all gods beside, give aid.

Such are my prayers; and over them I pour these drink
offerings.

(To the Chorus.)

Yours the mode now, yours to make these flower   150
with fierce laments, and incantation for the dead.

CHORUS [*singing*]
Let the tear fall, that clashes as it dies
as died our fallen lord;
die on this mound that fences good from evil,
washing away the death stain accursed   155
of drink offerings shed. Hear me, oh hear, my lord,
majesty hear me from your dark heart; oh hear,
oh oh!
Let one come, in strength
of spear, some man at arms who will set free the house   160
holding the Scythian bow backbent in his hands,
a mighty god of war spattering arrows
or closing to combat, with sword hilted fast to his hand.

ELECTRA
Father, the earth has drunk my offerings poured to you.   165
But something has happened here, my women. Help me now.

CHORUS LEADER
Speak, if you will. My heart is in a dance of fear.

ELECTRA
Someone has cut a strand of hair and laid it on
the tomb.

CHORUS LEADER
What man? Or was it some slim-waisted girl?

ELECTRA
There is a mark, which makes it plain for any to guess.   170

CHORUS LEADER
Explain, and let your youth instruct my greater age.

ELECTRA

No one could have cut off this strand, except myself.

CHORUS LEADER

Those others, for whom it were proper, are full of hate.

ELECTRA

Yet here it is, and for appearance matches well . . .

CHORUS LEADER

With whose hair? Tell me. This is what I long to know . . .   175

ELECTRA

With my own hair. It is almost exactly like.

CHORUS LEADER

Can it then be a secret gift from Orestes?

ELECTRA

It seems that it must be nobody's hair but his.

CHORUS LEADER

Did Orestes dare to come back here? How could this be?

ELECTRA

He sent it, this severed strand, to do my father honor.   180

CHORUS LEADER

It will not stop my tears if you are right. You mean
that he can never again set foot upon this land.

ELECTRA

The bitter wash has surged upon my heart as well.
I am struck through, as by the cross-stab of a sword,
and from my eyes the thirsty and unguarded drops   185
burst in a storm of tears like winter rain, as I
look on this strand of hair. How could I think some other
man, one of the citizens, could ever be lord of hair like this?
She never could have cut it, she who murdered him
and is my mother, but no mother in her heart   190
which has assumed god's hate and hates her children. No.

And yet, how can I say in open outright confidence
this is a treasured token from the best beloved
of men to me, Orestes? Does hope fawn on me?
Ah
I wish it had the kind voice of a messenger   195
so that my mind would not be torn in two, I not
shaken, but it could tell me plain to throw this strand°
away as trash, if it was cut from a hated head,
or like a brother could have mourned with me, and been
a treasured splendor for my father, and his grave.   200
     The gods know, and we call upon the gods; they know
how we are spun in circles like seafarers, in
what storms. But if we are to win, and our ship live,
from one small seed could burgeon an enormous tree.
But see, here is another sign. Footprints are here.   205
The feet that made them are alike, and look like mine.
There are two sets of footprints: of the man who gave
his hair, and one who shared the road with him. I step
where he has stepped, and heelmarks, and the space between
his heel and toe are like the prints I make. Oh, this   210
is torment, and my wits are going.

(Orestes comes forward from his place of concealment.)

ORESTES

Pray for what is to come, and tell the gods that they
have brought your former prayers to pass. Pray for success.

ELECTRA

Upon what ground? What have I won yet from the gods?

ORESTES

You have come in sight of all you long since prayed to see.   215

ELECTRA

How do you know what man was subject of my prayer?

ORESTES

I know about Orestes, how he stirred your heart.

ELECTRA

Yes; but how am I given an answer to my prayers?

ORESTES

Look at me. Look for no one closer to you than I.

ELECTRA

Is this some net of treachery you catch me in, stranger?   220

ORESTES

Then I must be contriving plots against myself.

ELECTRA

It is your pleasure to laugh at my unhappiness.

ORESTES

I only mock my own then, if I laugh at you.

ELECTRA

Are you really Orestes? Can I call you by that name?

ORESTES

You see my actual self and are slow to learn. And yet   225
you saw this strand of hair I cut in sign of grief
and shuddered with excitement, for you thought you saw
me, and again when you were measuring my tracks.
Now lay the severed strand against where it was cut
and see how well your brother's hair matches my head.°   230
Look at this piece of weaving, the work of your hand
with its blade strokes and figured design of beasts. No, no,
control yourself, and do not lose your head for joy.
I know those nearest to us hate us bitterly.

ELECTRA

O dearest, treasured darling of my father's house,   235
hope of the seed of our salvation, wept for, trust
your strength of hand, and win your father's house again.
O bright beloved presence, you bring back four lives
to me. To call you father is constraint of fact,
and all the love I could have borne my mother turns   240
your way, while she is loathed as she deserves; my love

for a pitilessly slaughtered sister turns to you.
And now you were my steadfast brother after all.
You alone bring me honor; but may Force, and Right,
and Zeus almighty, third with them, be on your side.°   245

ORESTES

Zeus, Zeus, gaze on all that we try to do. Behold
the orphaned children of the eagle-father, now
that he has died entangled in the twisting coils
of the deadly viper, and the young he left behind
are worn with the wasting of starvation, not full grown   250
to bring home to their nest the prey as their father did.
I, with my sister, whom I name, Electra here,
stand in your sight, children whose father is lost. We both
are driven in exile from the house that should be ours.
If you destroy these father's fledglings who gave you°   255
sacrifice and high honor, from what hand like his
shall you be given the sacred feast which is your right?
Destroy the eagle's brood, and you have no more means
to send your signs to mortals for their strong belief;
nor, if the stump rot through on this our royal tree,   260
shall it sustain your altars on sacrificial days.
Safe keep it: from a little thing you can raise up
a house to grandeur, though it now seem overthrown.

CHORUS

O children, silence! Saviors of your father's house,
be silent, children. Otherwise someone may hear   265
and for mere love of gossip carry news of all
you do, to those in power, to those I long to see
some day as corpses in the bubbling pitch and flame.

ORESTES

The big strength of Apollo's oracle will not
forsake me. For he charged me to win through this hazard,   270
with divination of much, and speech articulate,
warning of chill disaster under my warm heart
were I to fail against my father's murderers;

told me to cut them down in their own fashion, turn
to bull-like fury in the loss of my estates.   275
He said that else I must myself pay penalty
with my own life, and suffer much grim punishment;
spoke of the angers that come out of the ground from those
beneath who turn against men; spoke of sicknesses,
ulcers that ride upon the flesh, and cling, and with   280
wild teeth eat away the natural tissue, how on this
disease shall grow in turn a leprous fur. He spoke
of other ways again by which the Avengers might
attack, brought to fulfillment from my father's blood.
There's a dark weapon of those dead men underground   285
all those within my family who fell turn to call
upon me; madness and empty terror in the night
on one who sees clear those visions in the dark:
they tear him loose and shake him until, with all his body
degraded by the collar of bronze, he flees his city.°   290
And such as he can have no share in the communal bowl
allowed them, no cup filled for friends to drink. The wrath
of the father comes unseen on them to drive them back
from altars. None can take them in nor shelter them.
Dishonored and unloved by all the man must die   295
at last, shrunken and wasted away in painful death.
     Shall I not trust such oracles as this? Even if
I do not trust them, here is work that must be done.
Here numerous desires converge to drive me on:
the god's urgency and grief for my father, and with these   300
the loss of my estates wears hard on me; also
the thought that these my citizens, most high renowned
of men, who toppled Troy with hearts of valor, must
go subject to this pair of women; since "his" heart
is really female; or, if not, that soon will show.   305

CHORUS [*chanting*]
   Almighty Destinies, by the will
   of Zeus let these things

be done, in the turning of Justice.
In return for the word of hatred spoken, let hate
be a word fulfilled. The spirit of Right   310
cries out aloud and extracts atonement
due: blood stroke for the stroke of blood
shall be paid. Who acts, shall suffer. So speaks
the voice of the age-old wisdom.

ORESTES° [*singing throughout this lyric interchange with Electra and
the Chorus*]

STROPHE A

Father, O my dread father, what thing   315
can I say, can I accomplish
from this far place where I stand, to mark
and reach you there in your chamber
with light that will match your dark?
Yet it is called an action   320
of grace to mourn in style for the house,
once great, of the sons of Atreus.

CHORUS [*singing*]

STROPHE B

Child, when the fire burns
and tears with its teeth at the dead man   325
it cannot wear out the proud spirit.
He shows his wrath in the after-
days. One dies, and is lamented.
Light falls on the man who killed him.
He is hunted down by the deathsong
for sires slain and for fathers,   330
disturbed, and stern, and avenging.

ELECTRA [*singing throughout this lyric interchange*]

ANTISTROPHE A

Hear me, my father; hear in turn
all the tears of my sorrows.
Two children stand at your tomb to sing

the burden of your death chant.   335
Your grave is shelter to suppliants,
shelter to the outdriven.
What here is good; what escape from grief?
Can we outwrestle disaster?

CHORUS [*chanting*]
Yet from such as this the god, if he will,   340
can work out strains that are fairer.
For dirges chanted over the grave,
the winner's song in the royal house;
bring home to new arms the beloved.

ORESTES
                    STROPHE C
If only at Ilium,   345
father, and by some Lycian's hands
you had gone down at the spear's stroke,
you would have left high fame in your house,
for your children seen in the streets
admiration from all;   350
your tomb would be a deep piled bank of earth
founded in a land across the sea,
a light burden for your household;

CHORUS [*singing*]
                    ANTISTROPHE B
loved then by those he loved
down there beneath the ground   355
who died as heroes, he would have held
state, and a lord's majesty,
vassal only to those most great,
the kings of the underdarkness.
For he was king on earth when he lived°   360
over those whose hands held power of life
and death, and the staff of authority.

ELECTRA

No, but not under Troy's
ramparts, father, should you have died,
nor, with the rest of the spearstruck hordes   365
have found your grave by Scamandrus' crossing.
Sooner, his murderers
should have been killed, as he was,
by those they loved, and have found their death,
and people remote from this outrage   370
had heard the distant story.

CHORUS [*chanting*]

Child, child, you are dreaming, and dreaming is a light
pastime, of fortune more golden than gold
or the Blessed Ones north of the North Wind.
But the stroke of the twofold lash is pounding   375
close. Helpers are gathering underground
for some of us, while the hands of those who rule
are unclean, and these are accursed.
Power grows on the side of the children.°

ORESTES

STROPHE D

This cry has come to my ear   380
like a deep-driven arrow.
Zeus, Zeus, send up from below
ground the delayed destruction
on the cruel heart and the all-daring
hand, for the right of our fathers.   385

CHORUS [*singing*]

STROPHE E

May I claim the right to close the deathsong°
chanted in glory across
the man speared and the woman
dying. Why hide what deep within my breast always   390

flitters? Long since against the heart's
stem a bitter wind has blown
fierce anger and burdened hatred.

ELECTRA

ANTISTROPHE D

May Zeus, from all shoulder's strength,
pound down his fist upon them,   395
ah, ah! smash their heads.
Let the land once more believe.
There has been wrong done. I ask for right.
Hear me, Earth. Hear me, grandeurs of Darkness.

CHORUS [*chanting*]

It is but law that when the red drops have been spilled   400
upon the ground they cry aloud for fresh
blood. For the death act calls out on Fury
to bring up from those who were slain before
new ruin on ruin accomplished.

ORESTES

STROPHE F

Hear me, you lordships of the world below.   405
Behold in assembled power, curses come from the dead,
behold the last of the sons of Atreus, foundering
lost, without future, cast
from house and right. O Zeus, where shall we turn?

CHORUS [*singing throughout the rest of this lyric interchange*]

ANTISTROPHE E

The heart jumps in me once again   410
to hear this piteous prayer.
Disconsolate then was I
and now my heart darkens within
deep down, to hear you speak it.   415
But when strength came back hope lifted
me again, and the sorrow
was gone and the light was on me.°

ELECTRA

Of what thing can we speak, and strike more close,
than of the sorrows they who bore us have given?
So let her fawn if she likes. It softens not.   420
For we are bloody like the wolf
and savage born from the savage mother.

CHORUS

I struck my breast in the stroke-style of the Arian,
the Cissian mourning woman,
and the hail-beat of the drifting fists was there to see   425
as the rising pace went in a pattern of blows
downward and upward until the crashing strokes
played on my hammered, my all-stricken head.

ELECTRA

O cruel, cruel
all-daring mother, in cruel processional   430
with all his citizens gone,
with all sorrow for him forgotten
you dared bury your unbewept lord.

ORESTES

O all unworthy of him, what you tell me.
Shall she not pay for this dishonor   435
for all the immortals,
for all my own hands can do?
Let me but take her life and die for it.

CHORUS

Know then, they hobbled him beneath the armpits,
with his own hands. She wrought so, in his burial   440
to make his death a burden

beyond your strength to carry.
The mutilation of your father. Hear it.

ELECTRA

ANTISTROPHE G

You tell of how my father was murdered. Meanwhile I
stood apart, dishonored, nothing worth,   445
in the dark corner, as you would kennel a vicious dog,
and burst in an outrush of tears, that came that day
where smiles would not, and hid the streaming of my grief.
Hear such, and carve the letters of it on your heart.   450

CHORUS

ANTISTROPHE H

Let words such as these
drip deep in your ears, but on a quiet heart.
So far all stands as it stands;
what is to come, yourself burn to know.
You must be hard, give no ground, to win home.   455

ORESTES

STROPHE K

I speak to you. Be with those you love, my father.

ELECTRA

And I, all in my tears, ask with him.

CHORUS

We gather into murmurous revolt. Hear
us, hear. Come back into the light.
Be with us against those we hate.   460

ORESTES

ANTISTROPHE K

War-strength shall collide with war-strength; right with right.

ELECTRA

O gods, be just in what you bring to pass.

CHORUS
    My flesh crawls as I listen to them pray.
   The day of doom has waited long.
   They call for it. It may come.   465

STROPHE L

O pain grown into the race
and blood-dripping stroke
and grinding cry of disaster,
moaning and impossible weight to bear.
Sickness that fights all remedy.   470

ANTISTROPHE L

Here in the house resides
the cure for this, not to be brought
from outside, never from others
but within themselves, through the raw brutal bloodshed.
Here is the song sung to the gods beneath us.   475

[*chanting*]
Hear then, you blessed ones under the ground,
and answer these prayers with strength on our side,
free gift for your children's conquest.

ORESTES [*now speaking*]
   Father, O King who died no kingly death, I ask
   the gift of lordship at your hands, to rule your house.   480

ELECTRA [*speaking*]
   I too, my father, ask of you such grace as this:
   to murder Aegisthus with strong hand, and then go free.°

ORESTES
   So shall your memory have the feasts that men honor
   in custom. Otherwise at the tables when offerings
   burn for the earth, you shall be there, but none give heed.   485

ELECTRA
   I too out of my own full dowry then shall bring

libations for my bridal from my father's house.
Of all tombs, yours shall be the lordliest in my eyes.

ORESTES

O Earth, let my father emerge to watch me fight.

ELECTRA

Persephone, grant still the wonder of success. 490

ORESTES

Think of that bath, father, where you were stripped of life.

ELECTRA

Think of the casting net that they contrived for you.

ORESTES

They caught you like a beast in toils no bronzesmith made.

ELECTRA

Rather, hid you in shrouds that were thought out in shame.

ORESTES

Will you not waken, father, to these reproaches? 495

ELECTRA

Will you not raise upright that best beloved head?

ORESTES

Send out your Right to battle on the side of those
you love, or give us holds like those they caught you in.
For they threw you. Would you not see them thrown in turn?

ELECTRA

Hear one more cry, father, from me. It is my last. 500
Your nestlings huddle suppliant at your tomb: look forth
and pity them, female with the male strain alike.

ORESTES°

Do not wipe out this seed of the Pelopidae.
So, though you died, you shall not yet be dead, for when
a man dies, children are the voice of his salvation 505

afterward. Like corks upon the net, these hold
the drenched and flaxen meshes, and they will not drown.
Hear us, then. Our complaints are for your sake, and if
you honor this our argument, you save yourself.

CHORUS LEADER

None can find fault with the length of this discourse you drew   510
out, to show honor to a grave and fate unwept
before. The rest is action. Since your heart is set
that way, now you must strike and prove your destiny.

ORESTES

So. But I am not wandering from my strict course
when I ask why she sent these libations, for what cause   515
she acknowledges, too late, a crime for which there is
no cure. Here was a wretched grace brought to a man°
dead and unfeeling. This I fail to understand.
The offerings are too small for the act done. Pour out
all your possessions to atone one act of blood,   520
you waste your work, it is all useless, reason says.
Explain me this, for I would learn it, if you know.

CHORUS LEADER

I know, child, I was there. It was the dreams she had.
The godless woman had been shaken in the night
by floating terrors, when she sent these offerings.   525

ORESTES

Do you know the dream, too? Can you tell it to me right?

CHORUS LEADER

She told me herself. She dreamed she gave birth to a snake.

ORESTES

What is the end of the story then? What is the point?

CHORUS LEADER

She wrapped it warm in clothing as if it were a child.

ORESTES

A little monster. Did it want some kind of food?   530

CHORUS LEADER

She herself, in the dream, gave it her breast to suck.

ORESTES

How was her nipple not torn by such a beastly thing?

CHORUS LEADER

It was. The creature drew in blood along with the milk.

ORESTES

No vapid dream this. A man is the vision's subject.°

CHORUS LEADER

She woke screaming out of her sleep, shaky with fear,   535
as torches were kindled all about the house, out of
the blind dark that had been on them, to comfort the queen.
So now she sends these mourning offerings to be poured
and hopes they are medicinal for her disease.

ORESTES

But I pray to the earth and to my father's grave   540
that this dream is for me and that I will succeed.
See, I divine it, and it coheres all in one piece.
If this snake came out of the same place whence I came,
if she wrapped it in robes, as she wrapped me, and if
its jaws gaped wide around the breast that suckled me,   545
and if it stained the intimate milk with an outburst
of blood, so that for fright and pain she cried aloud,
it follows then, that as she nursed this hideous thing
of prophecy, she must be cruelly murdered. I
turn snake to kill her. This is what the dream speaks loud.   550

CHORUS LEADER

I choose you my interpreter to read these dreams.
So may it happen. Now you must rehearse your side
in their parts. For some, this means the parts they must not
    play.

ORESTES

Simple to tell them. My sister here must go inside.

I charge her to keep secret what we have agreed,   555
so that, as they by treachery killed a man of high
degree, by treachery tangled in the self-same net
they too shall die, in the way Loxias has ordained,
my lord Apollo, whose word was never false before.
Disguised as an outlander, for which I have all gear,   560
I shall go to the outer gates with Pylades
whom you see here. He is hereditary friend
and companion-in-arms of my house. We two shall both
    assume
the Parnassian dialect and imitate the way
they talk in Phocis. If none at the door will take us in   565
kindly, because the house is in a curse of ills,
we shall stay there, till anybody who goes by
the house will wonder why we are shut out, and say:
"Why does Aegisthus keep the suppliant turned away
from his gates, if he is hereabouts and knows of this?"   570
But if I once cross the doorstone of the outer gates
and find my man seated upon my father's throne,
or if he comes down to confront me, and uplifts
his eyes to mine, then lets them drop again, be sure,
before he can say: "Where does the stranger come from?" I   575
shall plunge my sword with lightning speed, and drop him
    dead.
Our Fury who is never starved for blood shall drink
for the third time a cupful of unwatered blood.
    Electra, keep a careful eye on all within
the house, so that our plans will hold together.

                                        (To the Chorus.)

                                        You,   580
women: I charge you, hold your tongues religiously.
Be silent if you must, or speak in the way that will
help us. And now I call upon the god who stands
close, to look on, and guide the actions of my sword.

(Exit Orestes and Pylades to the side, Electra into the palace.)

CHORUS [*singing*]

STROPHE A

Numberless, the earth breeds   585
dangers, and the awful thought of fear.
The bending sea's arms swarm
with bitter, savage beasts.
Torches blossom to burn along
the high space between ground and sky.   590
Things fly, and things walk the earth.
Remember too
the storm and wrath of the whirlwind.

ANTISTROPHE A

But who can recount all
the high daring in the will   595
of man, and in the stubborn hearts of women
the all-adventurous passions
that couple with man's overthrow.
The female force, the desperate
love crams its resisted way
on marriage and the dark embrace   600
of brute beasts, of mortal men.

STROPHE B

Let him, who goes not on flimsy wings
of thought, learn from her.
Althaea, Thestius'   605
daughter: who maimed her child, and hard
of heart, in deliberate guile
set fire to the bloody torch, her own son's
age-mate, that from the day he emerged
from the mother's womb crying   610
shared the measure of all his life
down to the marked death day.

And in the legends there is one more, a girl
of blood, figure of hate
who, for the enemy's
sake killed one near in blood, seduced by the wrought   615
golden necklace from Crete,
wherewith Minos bribed her. She sundered
from Nisus his immortal hair   620
as he all unsuspecting
breathed in a tranquil sleep. Foul wretch,
Hermes of death has got her now.

STROPHE C

Since I recall cruelties from quarrels long
ago, in vain, and married love turned to bitterness
a house would fend far away   625
by curse; the guile, treacheries of the woman's heart
against a lord armored in
power, a lord his enemies revered,°
I prize the hearth not inflamed within the house,
the woman's right pushed not into daring.   630

ANTISTROPHE C

Of all foul things told in legend the Lemnian
outranks, a vile wizard's charm, detestable
so that men name a hideous
crime "Lemnian" in memory of that wickedness.
When once the gods loathe a breed   635
of men they go outcast and forgotten.
No man respects what the gods have turned against.
What of these tales I gather has no meaning?

STROPHE D

The sword edges near the lungs.
It stabs deep, bittersharp,   640
and Right drives it. For that which had no right

lies not yet stamped into the ground, although
one in sin transgressed Zeus' majesty.   645

ANTISTROPHE D

Right's anvil stands staunch on the ground
and the smith, Destiny, hammers out the sword.
Delayed in glory, pensive from
the murk, Vengeance brings home at last   650
a child, to wipe out the stain of blood shed long ago.

> (Enter Orestes and Pylades from the side, carrying
> baggage and dressed as travelers.)

ORESTES

In there! Inside! Does anyone hear me knocking at
the gate? I will try again. Is anyone at home?
Try a third time. I ask for someone to come from the house,   655
if Aegisthus lets it welcome friendly visitors.

SERVANT   (Inside.)

All right, I hear you. Where does the stranger come from,
    then?

ORESTES

Announce me to the masters of the house. It is
to them I come, and I have news for them to hear.
And be quick, for the darkening chariot of night   660
leans to its course; the hour for wayfarers to drop
anchor in some place that entertains all travelers.
Have someone of authority in the house come out,
the lady of the place or, more appropriately,
its lord, for then no delicacy in speaking blurs   665
the spoken word. A man takes courage and speaks out
to another man, and makes clear everything he means.

> (Enter Clytaemestra from inside the palace.)

CLYTAEMESTRA

Friends, tell me only what you would have, and it is yours.
We have all comforts that go with a house like ours,

hot baths, and beds to charm away your weariness   670
with rest, and the regard of honest eyes. But if
you have some higher business, more a matter of state,
that is the men's concern, and I will tell them of it.

ORESTES

I am a Daulian stranger out of Phocis. As
I traveled with my pack and my own following   675
making for Argos, where my feet are rested now,
I met a man I did not know, nor did he know
me, but he asked what way I took, and told me his.
It was a Phocian, Strophius; for he told me his name
and said: "Friend, since in any case you make for Argos,   680
remember carefully to tell Orestes' parents
that he is dead; please do not let it slip your mind.
Then, if his people decide to have him brought back home,
or bury him where he went to live, all outlander   685
forever, carry their requests again to me.
For as it is, the bronze walls of an urn close in
the ashes of a man who has been deeply mourned."
So much I know, no more. But whether I now talk
with those who have authority and concern in this
I do not know. I think his father should be told.   690

CLYTAEMESTRA

Ah me. You tell us how we are stormed from head to heel.
Oh curse upon our house, bitter antagonist,
how far your eyes range. What was clean out of your way
your archery brings down with a distant deadly shot
to strip unhappy me of all I ever loved.   695
Even Orestes now! He was so well advised
to keep his foot clear of this swamp of death. But now
set down as traitor the hope that was our healer once
and made us look for a bright revel in our house.

ORESTES

I could have wished, with hosts so prosperous as you,   700
to have made myself known by some more gracious news

and so been entertained by you. For what is there
more kindly than the feeling between host and guest?
Yet it had been abuse of duty in my heart
had I not given so great a matter to his friends,   705
being so bound by promise and the stranger's rights.

CLYTAEMESTRA
You shall not find that your reception falls below
your worth, nor be any the less our friend for this.
Some other would have brought the news in any case.
But it is the hour for travelers who all day have trudged   710
the long road, to be given the rest that they deserve.
Escort this gentleman with his companion and
his men, to where our male friends are made at home.
Look after them, in manner worthy of a house
like ours; you are responsible for their good care.   715
Meanwhile, we shall communicate these matters to
the masters of the house, and with our numerous friends
deliberate the issues of this fatal news.

                              (Exit all but the Chorus, into the palace.)

CHORUS [chanting]
Handmaidens of this house, who help our cause,
how can our lips frame   720
some force that will show for Orestes?
    O Lady Earth, Earth Queen, who now
ride mounded over the lord of ships
where the king's corpse lies buried,
hear us, help us.   725
Now the time breaks for Persuasion in stealth
to go down to the Pit, with Hermes of death°
and the dark, to direct
trial by the sword's fierce edge.

CHORUS LEADER
I think our newcomer is at his deadly work;   730
I see Orestes' old nurse coming forth, in tears.

(Enter the Nurse, Cilissa, from inside the palace.)

Now where are you going, Cilissa, through the palace gates,
with sorrow as your hireless fellow wayfarer?

NURSE

The woman who is our mistress told me to make haste
and summon Aegisthus for the strangers, "so that he   735
can come and hear, as man to man, in more detail
this news that they have brought." She put a sad face on
before the servants, to hide the smile inside her eyes
over this work that has been done so happily
for her—though on this house the misery is now complete   740
from the plain story that the stranger men have brought.
But as for that Aegisthus, oh, he will be pleased
enough to hear the story. Poor unhappy me,
all my long-standing mixture of misfortunes, hard
burden enough, here in this house of Atreus,   745
when it befell me made the heart ache in my breast.
But never yet did I have to bear a hurt like this.
I took the other troubles bravely as they came:
but now, darling Orestes! I wore out my life
for him. I took him from his mother, brought him up.   750
There were times when he screamed at night and woke me
    from
my rest; I had to do many hard tasks, and now
useless; a baby is like a beast, it does not think
but you have to nurse it, do you not, the way it wants.
For the child still in swaddling clothes cannot tell us   755
if he is hungry or thirsty, if he needs to make
water. Children's young insides are a law to themselves.
I needed second sight for this, and many a time
I think I missed, and had to wash the baby's clothes.
The nurse and laundrywoman had a combined duty   760
and that was I. I was skilled in both handicrafts,
and so Orestes' father gave him to my charge.
And now, unhappy, I am told that he is dead

and go to take the story to that man who has
defiled our house; he will be glad to hear such news.   765

CHORUS LEADER

Did she say he should come back armed in any way?

NURSE

How, armed? Say it again. I do not understand.

CHORUS LEADER

Was he to come with bodyguards, or by himself?

NURSE

She said to bring his followers, the men-at-arms.

CHORUS LEADER

Now, if you hate our master, do not tell him that,   770
but simply bid him come as quickly as he can
and cheerfully. In that way he will not take fright.
It is the messenger who makes the bent word straight.

NURSE

But are you happy over what I have told you?

CHORUS LEADER

Perhaps: if Zeus might turn our evil wind to good.   775

NURSE

How so? Orestes, once hope of the house, is gone.

CHORUS LEADER

Not yet. It would be a poor seer who saw it thus.

NURSE

What is this? Have you some news that has not been told?

CHORUS LEADER

Go on and take your message, do as you were bid.
The gods' concerns are what concern only the gods.   780

NURSE

I will go then and do all this as you have told
me to. May all be for the best. So grant us god.

(Exit the Nurse to the side.)

CHORUS [*singing*]

STROPHE A

Now to my supplication. Zeus,
father of Olympian gods,
grant that those who struggle hard to see   785
temperate things done in the house win their aim°
in full. All that I spoke
was spoken in right. Yours, Zeus, to protect.

MESODE

Zeus, Zeus, make him who is now
in the house stand above those who
hate. If you rear him to greatness,   790
double and three times
and blithely he will repay you.

ANTISTROPHE A

See the colt of this man whom you loved
harnessed to the chariot   795
of suffering. Set upon the race he runs
sure control. Make us not see him break
stride, but clean down the course
keep the pace of his striding speed.

STROPHE B

You that, deep in the house   800
sway their secret pride of wealth,
hear us, gods of sympathy.
For things done in time past°
wash out the blood in fair-spoken verdict.   805
Let the old murder in
the house breed no more.

MESODE

And you, who keep, magnificent, the hallowed and huge
cavern, O grant that the man's house lift up its head

and look on the shining of daylight
and liberty with eyes made 810
glad with gazing out from the helm of darkness.

And with Right may the son
of Maia lend his hand, strong to send
wind fair for action, if he will.
Much else lies secret he may show at need. 815
He speaks the secret word, by
night hoods darkness on the eyes
nor shows more plainly when the day is there.

Then at last we shall sing
for deliverance of the house 820
the woman's song that sets the wind
fair, no thin-drawn and grief-
struck wail, but this: "The ship sails fair."
My way, mine, the advantage piles here, with wreck 825
and ruin far from those I love.

Be not fear-struck when your turn comes in the action,
but with a great cry "Father"
when she cries "Child" to you
go on through with the innocent murder. 830

Yours to raise high within
your body the heart of Perseus
and for those under the ground you loved
and those yet above, to exact
what their bitter passion may desire; make 835
bloody ruin of the Gorgon inside the house;°
wipe out the man stained with murder.

(Enter Aegisthus from the side, alone.)

AEGISTHUS

It is not without summons that I come, but called
by messenger, with news that there are strangers here
arrived, telling a story that brings no delight: 840
the death of Orestes. For our house, already bitten
and poisoned, to take this new load upon itself
would be a thing of dripping fear and blood. Yet how
shall I pass upon these rumors? As the living truth?
For messages made out of women's terror leap   845
high in the upward air and empty die. Do you
know anything of this by which to clear my mind?

CHORUS LEADER

We heard, yes. But go on inside and hear it from
the strangers. Messengers are never quite so sure
as a man's questions answered by the men themselves.   850

AEGISTHUS

I wish to question, carefully, this messenger
and learn if he himself was by when the man died
or if he heard but some blind rumor and so speaks.
The mind has eyes, not to be easily deceived.

(Aegisthus goes inside.)

CHORUS [chanting]

Zeus, Zeus, what shall I say, where make   855
a beginning of prayer for the gods' aid?
My will is good
but how shall I speak to match my need?
The bloody edges of the knives that rip   860
man-flesh are moving to work. It will mean
utter and final ruin imposed
on Agamemnon's
house, or our man will kindle a flame
and light of liberty, win the domain
and huge treasure again of his fathers.   865
Forlorn challenger, though blessed by god,

Orestes must come to grips with two,
so wrestle. Yet may he throw them.

(A shriek is heard from inside the house.)

[singing]
Listen, it goes   870
but how? What has been done in the house?

CHORUS LEADER [speaking]
Stand we aside until the work is done, for so
we shall not seem to be accountable in this
foul business. For the fight is done, the issue drawn.

(Enter a Follower of Aegisthus, running from inside the house.)

FOLLOWER
O sorrow, all is sorrow for our stricken lord.   875
Raise up again a triple cry of sorrow, for
Aegisthus lives no longer. Open there, open
quick as you may, and slide back the door bars on the
    women's
gates. It will take the strength of a young arm, but not
to fight for one who is dead and done for. What use there?   880
Ho there, ho!
My cry is to the deaf and I babble in vain
at sleepers to no purpose. Clytaemestra, where
is she, does what? Her neck is on the razor's edge
and ripe for lopping, as she did to others before.

(Enter Clytaemestra.)

CLYTAEMESTRA
What is this, and why are you shouting in the house?   885

FOLLOWER
I tell you, the living are being killed by the dead ones.

CLYTAEMESTRA
Ah, so. You speak in riddles, but I read the rhyme.

We have been won with the treachery by which we slew.
Bring me quick, somebody, an axe to kill a man

(Exit Follower.)

and we shall see if we can beat him before we   890
go down—so far gone are we in this wretched fight.

(Enter Orestes and Pylades from the palace, with swords drawn.)

ORESTES

You next: the other one in there has had enough.

CLYTAEMESTRA

Beloved, strong Aegisthus, are you dead indeed?

ORESTES

You love your man, then? You shall lie in the same grave
with him, and never be unfaithful even in death.   895

CLYTAEMESTRA

Hold, my son. Oh take pity, child, before this breast
where many a time, a drowsing baby, you would feed
and with soft gums sucked in the milk that made you strong.

ORESTES

What shall I do, Pylades? Be shamed to kill my mother?

PYLADES

What then becomes thereafter of the oracles   900
declared by Loxias at Pytho? What of sworn oaths?
Count all men hateful to you rather than the gods.

ORESTES

I judge that you win. Your advice is good.

(To Clytaemestra.)

Come here.

My purpose is to kill you over his body.
You thought him bigger than my father while he lived.   905
Die then and sleep beside him, since he is the man
you love, and he you should have loved got only your hate.

CLYTAEMESTRA

I raised you when you were little. May I grow old with you?

ORESTES

You killed my father. Would you make your home with me?

CLYTAEMESTRA

Destiny had some part in that, my child.   910

ORESTES

                                                            Why then
destiny has worked this death for you as well.

CLYTAEMESTRA

A mother has her curse, child. Are you not afraid?

ORESTES

No. You bore me and threw me away, to a hard life.

CLYTAEMESTRA

I sent you to a friend's house. This was no throwing away.

ORESTES

I was born of a free father. You sold me.   915

CLYTAEMESTRA

So? Where then is the price that I received for you?

ORESTES

I could say. It would be indecent to tell you.

CLYTAEMESTRA

Or if you do, tell also your father's follies.

ORESTES

Blame him not. He suffered while you were sitting here at
    home.

CLYTAEMESTRA

It hurts women to be kept from their men, my child.   920

ORESTES

The man's hard work supports the women who sit at home.

CLYTAEMESTRA

I think, child, that you mean to kill your mother.

ORESTES

No.

It will be you who kill yourself. It will not be I.

CLYTAEMESTRA

Take care. Your mother's curse, like dogs, will drag you down.

ORESTES

How shall I escape my father's curse, if I fail here?   925

CLYTAEMESTRA

I feel like one who wastes live tears upon a tomb.

ORESTES

Yes, this is death, your wages for my father's fate.

CLYTAEMESTRA

You are the snake I gave birth to, and gave the breast.

ORESTES

Indeed, the terror of those dreams saw things to come
clearly.° You killed, and it was wrong. Now suffer wrong.   930

(Orestes and Pylades take Clytaemestra into the palace.)

CHORUS LEADER

I have sorrow even for this pair in their twofold
downfall. But since Orestes had the hardiness
to end this chain of bloodlettings, here lies our choice,
that the eyes' light in this house shall not utterly die.

CHORUS [singing]

STROPHE A

Justice came at the last to Priam and all his sons   935
and it was heavy and hard,
but into the house of Agamemnon returned
the double lion, the double assault,
and the Pythian-steered exile

drove home to the hilt
vengeance, moving strongly in guidance sent by the god. 940

MESODE

Raise up the high cry O over our lordships' house
won free of distress, free of its fortunes wasted
by two stained with murder,
free of its mournful luck. 945

ANTISTROPHE A

He came back; his work lay in the secret attack
and it was stealthy and hard,
but in the fighting his hand was steered by the very daughter
of Zeus: Right we call her, 950
mortals who speak of her and name her well. Her wind
is fury and death visited upon those she hates.

STROPHE B

All that Loxias, who on Parnassus holds
the huge, the deep cleft in the ground, shrilled aloud,
by guile that is no guile 955
returns now to assault the wrong done and grown old.
Divinity keeps, we know not how, strength to resist
surrender to the wicked.
The power that holds the sky's majesty wins our worship. 960

MESODE

Light is here to behold.
The big bit that curbed our house is taken away.
Rise up, you halls, arise; for time grown too long
you lay tumbled along the ground.

ANTISTROPHE B

Time brings all things to pass. Presently time shall cross 965
the outgates of the house after the stain is driven
entire from the hearth
by ceremonies that wash clean and cast out the furies.
The dice of fortune shall be thrown once more, and lie

prosperous and smiling   970
up at the new indwellers come to live in the house.

> (The doors of the house open, to show Orestes standing over the
> bodies of Clytaemestra and Aegisthus, while attendants display
> the net-like garment in which Clytaemestra had entangled
> Agamemnon and which she herself displayed after his murder.)

ORESTES

Behold the twin tyrannies of our land, these two
who killed my father and who sacked my house. For a time
they sat upon their thrones and kept their pride of state,   975
and they are lovers still. So may you judge by what
befell them, for as they were pledged their oath abides.
They swore together death for my unhappy sire
and swore to die together. Now they keep their oath.
Behold again, O audience of these evil things,   980
the engine against my wretched father they devised,
the hands' entanglement, the hobbles for his feet.
Spread it out. Stand around me in a circle and
display this net that caught a man. So shall, not my
father, but that great father who sees all, the Sun,   985
look on my mother's sacrilegious handiwork
and be a witness for me in my day of trial
how it was in all right that I achieved this death,
my mother's: for of Aegisthus' death I take no count:
he has his seducer's punishment, no more than law.   990
But she, who plotted this foul death against the man
by whom she carried the weight of children underneath
her belt, burden once loved, shown hard and hateful now,
what does she seem to be? Some water snake, some viper
whose touch is rot even to him who felt no fang   995
strike, by that brutal and wrong daring in her heart.
And this thing: what shall I call it and be right, in all
eloquence? Trap for an animal or winding sheet
for a dead man? Or bath curtain? Since it is a net,
robe you could call it, to entangle a man's feet.   1000

Some highwayman might own a thing like this, to catch
the wayfarer and rob him of his money and
so make a living. With a treacherous thing like this
he could take many victims and warm his heart within.
May no such partner as she was come to live with me.   1005
Sooner, let god destroy me, with no children born.

CHORUS [*chanting*]
   Ah, but the pitiful work.
   Dismal the death that was your ending.
   He is left alive; pain flowers for him.

ORESTES
   Did she do it or did she not? My witness is
   this great robe. It was thus she stained Aegisthus' sword.   1010
   Dip it and dip it again, the smear of blood conspires
   with time to spoil the beauty of this precious thing.
   Now I can praise him, now I can stand by to mourn
   and speak before this web that killed my father; yet   1015
   I grieve for the thing done, the death, and all our race.
   I have won; but my victory is polluted, and has no pride.

CHORUS [*chanting*]
   There is no mortal man who shall turn
   unhurt his life's course to an end not marred.
   There is trouble here. There is more to come.   1020

ORESTES
   I would have you know, I see not how this thing will end.
   I am a charioteer whose course is wrenched outside
   the track, for I am beaten, my rebellious senses
   bolt with me headlong and the fear against my heart
   is ready for the singing and dance of wrath. But while   1025
   I hold some grip still on my wits, I say publicly
   to my friends: I killed my mother not without some right.
   My father's murder stained her, and the gods' disgust.
   As for the spells that charmed me to such daring, I   1030
   cite above all the seer of Pytho, Loxias. He

declared I could do this and not be charged with wrong,
while if I refused, the punishment I will not speak:
no archery could hit such height of agony.
And look upon me now, how I go armored in
leafed branch and garland on my way to the centerstone   1035
and sanctuary, and Apollo's sacred ground,
the shining of the fabulous fire that never dies,
to escape this blood that is my own. Loxias ordained
that I should turn me to no other shrine than this.
To all men of Argos in time to come I say   1040
they shall be witness, how these evil things were done.
I go, an outcast wanderer from this land, and leave
behind, in life, in death, the name of what I did.

CHORUS LEADER

No, what you did was well done. Do not therefore bind
your mouth to foul speech. Keep no evil on your lips.   1045
You liberated all the Argive city when
you lopped the heads of these two snakes with one clean
    stroke.

ORESTES

No!
Women who serve this house, they come like Gorgons, they
wear robes of black, and they are wreathed in a tangle
of snakes. I can no longer stay.   1050

CHORUS LEADER

Orestes, dearest to your father of all men,
what fancies whirl you? Hold, do not give way to fear.

ORESTES

These are no fancies of affliction. They are clear,
and real, and here; the bloodhounds of my mother's hate.

CHORUS LEADER

It is the blood still wet upon your hands, that makes   1055
this shaken turbulence be thrown upon your sense.

ORESTES

Ah, Lord Apollo, how they grow and multiply,
repulsive for the blood drops of their dripping eyes.

CHORUS LEADER

There is one way to make you clean: let Loxias
touch you, and set you free from these disturbances.   1060

ORESTES

You cannot see them, but I see them. I am driven
from this place. I can stay here no longer.

(*Exit, to the side.*)

CHORUS LEADER

Good luck go with you then, and may the god look on
you with favor and guard you in kind circumstance.

CHORUS [*chanting*]

Here on this house of the kings the third   1065
storm has broken, with wind
from the inward race, and gone its course.
The children were eaten: that was the first
affliction, the curse of Thyestes.
Next came the royal death, when a man   1070
and lord of Achaean armies went down
killed in the bath. Third
is for the savior. He came. Shall I call
it that, or death? Where
is the end? Where shall the fury of fate   1075
be stilled to sleep, be done with?

THE EUMENIDES

Characters   THE PYTHIAN PRIESTESS OF APOLLO
APOLLO
HERMES (silent character)
ORESTES, son of Agamemnon
GHOST of Clytaemestra
CHORUS of Furies (Eumenides)
ATHENA
JURYMEN (silent)
SECOND CHORUS, women of Athens

Scene: For the first part of the play (1–234) the scene is Delphi, in front of the sanctuary of Pythian Apollo. The action of the rest of the play (235 to the end) takes place at Athens, on the Acropolis in front of the temple of Athena.

(Enter the Pythian Priestess, from the side.)

PYTHIA

I give first place of honor in my prayer to her
who of the gods first prophesied, the Earth; and next
to Themis, who succeeded to her mother's place
of prophecy; so runs the legend; and in third
succession, given by free consent, not won by force,   5
another Titan daughter of Earth was seated here.
This was Phoebe. She gave it as a birthday gift
to Phoebus, who is called still after Phoebe's name.
And he, leaving the pond of Delos and the reef,
grounded his ship at the roadstead of Pallas, then   10

made his way to this land and a Parnassian home.
Deep in respect for his degree Hephaestus' sons
conveyed him here, for these are builders of roads, and changed
the wilderness to a land that was no wilderness.
He came so, and the people highly honored him,   15
with Delphus, lord and helmsman of the country. Zeus
made his mind full with godship and prophetic craft
and placed him, fourth in a line of seers, upon this throne.
So, Loxias is the spokesman of his father, Zeus.
These are the gods I set in the proem of my prayer.   20
But Pallas-before-the-temple has her right in all
I say. I worship the nymphs where the Corycian rock
is hollowed inward, haunt of birds and paced by gods.
Bromius, whom I forget not, sways this place. From here
in divine form he led his Bacchanals in arms   25
to hunt down Pentheus like a hare in the deathtrap.
I call upon the springs of Pleistus, on the power
of Poseidon, and on final loftiest Zeus,
then go to sit in prophecy on the throne. May all
grant me that this of all my entrances shall be   30
the best by far. If there are any Hellenes here
let them draw lots, so enter, as the custom is.
My prophecy is only as the god may guide.

> *(She enters the temple and almost immediately*
> *comes out again, crawling on all fours.)*

Things terrible to tell and for the eyes to see
terrible drove me out again from Loxias' house   35
so that I have no strength and cannot stand on springing
feet, but run with hands' help and my legs have no speed.
An old woman afraid is nothing: a child, no more.
See, I am on my way to the wreath-hung recess
and on the centerstone I see a man with god's   40
defilement on him postured in the suppliant's seat

with blood dripping from his hands and from a new-drawn
    sword,
holding too a branch that had grown high on an olive
tree, decorously wrapped in a great tuft of wool,
and the fleece shone. So far, at least, I can speak clear.   45
In front of this man slept a startling company
of women lying all upon the chairs. Or not
women, I think I call them rather Gorgons, only
not Gorgons either, since their shape is not the same.
I saw some creatures painted in a picture once,   50
who tore the food from Phineus, only these have no
wings, that could be seen; they are black and utterly
repulsive, and they snore with breath that drives one back.
From their eyes drips the foul ooze, and their dress is such
as is not right to wear in the presence of the gods'   55
statues, nor even in any human house.
I have never seen the tribe that spawned this company
nor know what piece of earth can claim with pride it bore
such brood, and without hurt and tears for labor given.
    Now after this the master of the house must take   60
his own measures: Apollo Loxias, who is very strong
and heals by divination, reads portentous signs,
and so purifies the houses others hold as well.

(Exit the Pythia. The doors of the temple open and show Orestes
surrounded by the sleeping Furies, Apollo and Hermes beside him.)

APOLLO

I will not give you up. Through to the end standing
your guardian, whether by your side or far away,   65
I shall not weaken toward your enemies. See now
how I have caught and overpowered these rabid creatures.
The repulsive maidens have been stilled to sleep, those gray
and aged children, they with whom no mortal man,
no god, nor even any beast, will have to do.   70
It was because of evil they were born, because

they hold the evil darkness of the Pit below
earth, loathed alike by men and by the heavenly gods.
Nevertheless, run from them, never weaken. They
will chase your track as you stride on across the long   75
land, and your driven feet forever pound the earth,
on across the main water and the circle-washed
cities. Be herdsman to this hard march. Never fail
until you come at last to Pallas' citadel.
Kneel there, and clasp the ancient idol in your arms,   80
and there we shall find those who will judge this case, and
    words
to say that will have magic in their figures. Thus
you will be rid of your afflictions, once for all.
For it was I who made you strike your mother down.

ORESTES

My lord Apollo, you understand what it means to do   85
no wrong. Learn also what it is not to neglect.
None can mistrust your power to do good, if you will.°

APOLLO

Remember: let not the fear overcome your heart.
Hermes, you are my brother from a single sire.
Look after him, and as you are named the god who guides,   90
be such in strong fact. He is my suppliant. Shepherd him
with fortunate escort on his journeys among men.
The wanderer has rights which Zeus acknowledges.

> (Exit Apollo into the temple, Orestes guided by Hermes
> to the side. Enter the Ghost of Clytaemestra.)

CLYTAEMESTRA

You would sleep, then? And what use are you, if you sleep?
It is because of you I go dishonored thus   95
among the rest of the dead. Because of those I killed
reproaches among the perished never cease for me
and I am driven in disgrace. I say to you

that I am charged with guilt most grave by these. And yet
I suffered too, horribly, and from those most dear,   100
yet none among the powers is angered for my sake
that I was slaughtered, and by matricidal hands.
Look at these gashes in my heart, think where they came
from. Eyes illuminate the sleeping brain,
but in the daylight man's future cannot be seen.°   105
Yet I have given you much to lap up, outpourings
without wine, sober propitiations, sacrificed
in secrecy of night and on a hearth of fire
for you, at an hour given to no other god.
Now I watch all these honors trampled into the ground,   110
and he is out and gone away like a hunted fawn
so lightly, from the very middle of your nets,
sprung clear, and laughing merrily at you. Hear me.
It is my life depends upon this spoken plea.
Think then, O goddesses beneath the ground. For I,   115
the dream of Clytaemestra, call upon your name.

(The Furies stir in their sleep and whimper.)

CLYTAEMESTRA

Oh, whimper, then, but your man has got away and gone
far. He has friends to help him, who are not like mine.   120

(They whimper again.)

CLYTAEMESTRA

Too much sleep and no pity for my plight. I stand,
his mother, here, killed by Orestes. He is gone.

(They moan in their sleep.)

CLYTAEMESTRA

You moan, you sleep. Get on your feet quickly, will you?
What have you yet got done, except to do evil?   125

(They moan again.)

CLYTAEMESTRA

Sleep and fatigue, two masterful conspirators,
have dimmed the deadly anger of the mother-snake.

(The Chorus start violently, then cry out in their sleep.)

CHORUS [*singing*]

Get him, get him, get him, get him! Make sure! 130

CLYTAEMESTRA

The beast you are after is a dream, but like the hound
whose thought of hunting has no lapse, you bay him on.
What are you about? Up, let not work's weariness
beat you, nor slacken with sleep so you forget my pain.
Scold your own heart and hurt it, as it well deserves, 135
for this is discipline's spur upon her own. Let go
upon this man the stormblasts of your bloodshot breath,
wither him in your wind, after him, hunt him down
once more, and shrivel him in your stomach's heat and flame.

*(Exit the Ghost. The Chorus begin to waken and
enter from the temple, one by one.)*

CHORUS LEADER

Waken. You are awake, wake her, as I did you. 140
You dream still? On your feet and kick your sleep aside.
Let us see whether this prelude was in vain.

CHORUS [*singing*]

STROPHE A

Sisters, we have had wrong done us.
When I have undergone so much and all in vain.
Suffering, suffering, bitter, oh shame shame, 145
unendurable wrong.
The hunted beast has slipped clean from our nets and gone.
Sleep defeated me, and I lost my prey.

ANTISTROPHE A

Shame, son of Zeus! Robber is all you are.
A young god, you have ridden down powers gray with age, 150

honored the suppliant, though a godless man, who hurt
the mother who gave him birth.
Yourself a god, you stole the matricide away.
Where in this act shall any man say there is right?

STROPHE B

The accusation came upon me from my dreams,   155
and hit me, as with a goad in the midgrip of his fist
the charioteer strikes,
but deep, beneath lobe and heart.
The public scourger's cutting whip is mine to feel   160
and the weight of pain is big, heavy to bear.

ANTISTROPHE B

Such are the actions of the younger gods. These occupy
by unconditional force, beyond all right, a throne
that runs reeking blood,
blood at the feet, blood at the head.   165
The very stone center of earth here in our eyes horrible
with blood and curse stands plain to see.

STROPHE C

Himself a seer, he has spoiled his secret shrine's
hearth with the stain, driven and hallooed the action on.   170
He made man's way cross the place of the ways of god
and blighted age-old distributions of power.

ANTISTROPHE C

He has wounded me, but he shall not get this man away.
Let him hide under the ground, he shall never go free.   175
Cursed suppliant, he shall feel against his head
another murderer rising out of the same seed.

(Enter Apollo again, from his sanctuary.)

APOLLO

Get out, I tell you, go and leave this house. Away
in haste, from your presence set the mantic chamber free,   180
else you may feel the flash and bite of a flying snake

launched from the twisted thong of gold that spans my bow
to make you in your pain spew out the black and foaming
blood of men, vomit the clots sucked from their veins.
This house is no right place for such as you to cling   185
upon; but where, by judgment given, heads are lopped
and eyes gouged out, throats cut, and by destruction of seed
the potency of boys is ruined,° where mutilation
lives, and stoning, and the long moan of tortured men
spiked underneath the spine and fixed on stakes. Listen   190
to how the gods spit out the manner of that feast
your appetites prefer. The whole way you look is guide
to what you are—the likes of whom should hole in the cave
of the blood-reeking lion, not wipe off your filth
on others nearby, in this oracular sanctuary.   195
Out then, you flock of goats without a herdsman, since
no god has such affection as to tend this herd.

CHORUS LEADER
My lord Apollo, it is your turn to listen now.
Your own part in this is more than accessory.
You are the one who did it; all the guilt is yours.   200

APOLLO
So? How? Continue speaking, until I understand.

CHORUS LEADER
You gave this outlander the word to kill his mother.

APOLLO
The word to exact price for his father. What of that?

CHORUS LEADER
You then dared take him in, fresh from his bloodletting.

APOLLO
Yes, and I told him to take refuge in this house.   205

CHORUS LEADER
Yet you abuse us, after we escorted him here?

APOLLO

Yes. It was not for you to come near this house.

CHORUS LEADER

And yet we have our duty—to do what we have done.

APOLLO

An office? You? Sound forth your glorious privilege.

CHORUS LEADER

This: to drive matricides out of their houses.   210

APOLLO

Then

what if it be the woman and she kills her husband?

CHORUS LEADER

Such murder would not be the shedding of kindred blood.

APOLLO

You have made into a thing of no account, no place,
the sworn faith of Zeus and of Hera, lady
of consummations, and Cypris by such argument   215
is thrown away, outlawed, and yet the sweetest things
in man's life come from her, for married love between
man and woman is bigger than oaths, guarded by right
of nature. If when such kill each other you are slack
so as not to take vengeance nor eye them in wrath,   220
then I deny your manhunt of Orestes goes
with right. I see that one cause moves you to strong rage
but on the other clearly you are unmoved to act.
Pallas divine shall review the pleadings of this case.

CHORUS LEADER

Nothing will ever make me let that man go free.   225

APOLLO

Keep after him then, and make more trouble for yourselves.

CHORUS LEADER

Do not try to curtail my privilege by argument.

APOLLO

I would not take your privilege if you gave it me.

CHORUS LEADER

No, for you are called great beside the throne of Zeus
already, but the motherblood drives me, and I go   230
to win my right upon this man and hunt him down.

APOLLO

But I shall give this suppliant help and rescue, for
if I willingly fail him who turns to me for aid,
his wrath, before gods and men, is a fearful thing.

*(Exit all separately. The scene is now Athens, on the Acropolis in
front of the temple and statue of Athena. Enter Orestes from the
side. He takes up a suppliant posture at the feet of the statue.)*

ORESTES

My lady Athena, it is at Loxias' behest   235
I come. So take in of your grace the wanderer
who comes, no suppliant, not unwashed of hand, but one
blunted at last, and worn and battered on the outland
habitations and the journeyings of men.
Crossing the dry land and the sea alike, keeping   240
the ordinances of Apollo's oracle
I come, goddess, before your statue and your house
to keep watch here and wait the issue of my trial.

(Enter the Chorus from the side.)

CHORUS LEADER

So. Here the man has left a clear trail behind; keep on,   245
keep on, as the unspeaking accuser tells us, by
whose sense, like hounds after a bleeding fawn, we trail
our quarry by the splash and drip of blood. And now
my lungs are blown with abundant and with wearisome
work, mankilling. My range has been the entire extent
of land, and, flown unwinged across the open water,   250

I am here, and give way to no ship in my pursuit.
Our man has gone to cover somewhere in this place.
The welcome smell of human blood has told me so.

CHORUS [*singing*]
Look again, look again,
search everywhere, let   255
not the matricide
steal away and escape.

(*They see Orestes.*)

See there! He clings to defense
again, his arms winding the immortal goddess'
image, so seeks acquittal out of our hands.   260
It shall not be. His mother's blood spilled on the ground
cannot come back again.
It is all soaked and drained into the ground and gone.

You must give back for her blood from the living man
red blood of your body to suck, and from your own   265
I could feed, with bitter-swallowed drench,
turn your strength limp while yet you live and drag you down
where you must pay for the pain of the murdered mother,
and watch the rest of the mortals stained with violence
against god or guest   270
or hurt parents who were close and dear,
each with the pain upon him that his crime deserves.
Hades is great, Hades calls men to reckoning
there under the ground,
sees all, and inscribes it deep in his recording mind.   275

ORESTES
I have been beaten and been taught, I understand
the many rules of absolution, where it is right
to speak and where be silent. In this action now
speech has been ordered by my teacher, who is wise.
The stain of blood dulls now and fades upon my hand.   280

My blot of matricide is being washed away.
When it was fresh still, at the hearth of the god, Phoebus,
it was absolved and driven out by sacrifice
of a pig, and the list were long if I went back to tell
of all I met who were not hurt by being with me.   285
Time in his aging overtakes all things alike.
Now it is from pure mouth and with good auspices
I call upon Athena, queen of this land, to come
and rescue me. She, without work of her spear, shall win
myself and all my land and all the Argive host   290
to stand her staunch companion for the rest of time.
Whether now ranging somewhere in the Libyan land
beside her father's crossing and by Triton's run
of waters she sets her foot upright or enshrouded
rescuing there her friends, or on the Phlegraean plain   295
like some bold man of armies sweeps with eyes the scene,
let her come! She is a god and hears me far away.
So may she set me free from what is at my back.

CHORUS LEADER

Neither Apollo nor Athena's strength can win
you free, save you from going down forgotten, without   300
knowing where joy lies anywhere inside your heart,
blood drained, chewed dry by the powers of death, a wraith,
    a shell.
You will not speak to answer, spew my challenge away?
You are consecrate to me and fattened for my feast,
and you shall feed me while you live, not cut down first   305
at the altar. Hear the spell I sing to bind you in.

CHORUS [chanting]

Come then, link we our choral dance.
Ours to show forth the power
and terror of our music, declare
our rights of office, how we conspire   310
to steer men's lives.
We hold we are straight and just. If a man

can spread his hands and show they are clean,
no wrath of ours shall lurk for him.
Unscathed he walks through his life time.   315
But one like this man before us, with stained
hidden hands, and the guilt upon him,
shall find us beside him, as witnesses
of the truth, and we show clear in the end
to avenge the blood of the murdered.   320

[singing]

STROPHE A

Mother, O my mother night, who gave me
birth, to be a vengeance on the seeing
and the blind, hear me. For Leto's
youngling takes my right away,
stealing from my clutch the prey   325
that cowers, whose blood would wipe
at last the motherblood away.

REFRAIN A

Over the beast doomed to the fire
this is the chant, scatter of wits,
frenzy and fear, hurting the heart,   330
song of the Furies
binding brain and blighting blood
in its stringless melody.

ANTISTROPHE A

This the purpose that all-involving
Destiny spun, to be ours and to be shaken   335
never: when mortals assume outrage
of their own hand in violence,
these we hound, till one goes
under earth. Nor does death
set them altogether free.   340

REFRAIN A

Over the beast doomed to the fire

this is the chant, scatter of wits,
frenzy and fear, hurting the heart,
song of the Furies
binding brain and blighting blood   345
in its stringless melody.

STROPHE B

When we were born such lots were assigned for our keeping.
So the immortals must hold hands off, nor is there   350
one of them who shall sit at our feasting.
In pure white robes I have no interest and no portion.°

REFRAIN B

I have chosen overthrow
of houses, where the battle god   355
grown within strikes near and dear
down. So we swoop upon this man
here. He is strong, but we wear him down
for the blood that is still wet on him.

ANTISTROPHE B

Being eager to save all others from these concerns   360
by our efforts we provide for the gods immunity,°
and no appeal comes to them,
since Zeus has ruled our blood-dripping company   365
outcast, nor will deal with us.

REFRAIN B

I have chosen overthrow
of houses, where the battle god
grown within strikes near and dear
down. So we swoop upon this man
here. He is strong, but we wear him down
for the blood that is still wet on him.

STROPHE C

Men's illusions in their pride under the sky melt
down, and are diminished into the ground, gone

before the onset of our black robes, and the dancing   370
of our vindictive feet against them.

For with a long leap from high
above and dead drop of weight
I bring foot's force crashing down
to cut the legs from under even   375
the runner, and spill him to ruin.

He falls, and does not know in the daze of his folly.
Such in the dark of man is the mist of infection
that hovers, and moaning rumor tells how his house lies
under fog that glooms above.   380

For with a long leap from high
above, and dead drop of weight,
I bring foot's force crashing down
to cut the legs from under even
the runner, and spill him to ruin.

All holds.° For we are strong and skilled;
we have authority; we hold
memory of evil; we are stern,
nor can men's pleadings bend us. We
accomplish our duties, spurned, outcast   385
from gods, standing apart in slime
unlit by the sun. Rocky and rough are the paths
for those who see and alike for those whose eyes are lost.

Is there a man who does not fear
this, does not shrink to hear   390
how my place has been ordained,
granted and given by destiny

and the gods, absolute? Privilege
primeval yet is mine, nor am I without place
though it be underneath the ground   395
and in no sunlight and in darkness that I must stand.

                              (Enter Athena, in full armor.)

ATHENA

From far away I heard the outcry of your call.
It was beside Scamandrus. I was taking claim
of land, for there the Achaean lords of war and first
fighters gave me large portion of all their spears   400
had won, the land root and stock to be mine for all
eternity, for the sons of Theseus a choice gift.
From there, sped on my weariless feet, I came, wingless
but in the rush and speed of the aegis fold.° And now
I see upon this land a strange new company   405
which, though it brings no terror to my eyes, brings still
wonder. Who are you? I address you all alike,
both you, the stranger kneeling at my image here,
and you, who are like no seed ever begotten, not   410
recognized by the gods as goddesses, nor yet
stamped in the likenesses of any human form.
But no. This is the place of the just. Its rights forbid
to speak evil of another who is without blame.

CHORUS LEADER

Daughter of Zeus, you shall hear all compressed to brief   415
measure. We are the eternal children of the Night.
Curses they call us in our homes beneath the ground.

ATHENA

I know your race, then, and the names by which you are
    called.

CHORUS LEADER

And soon you shall be told of our prerogatives.

ATHENA

I can know them, if someone will give me a clear account.   420

CHORUS LEADER

We drive from home those who have shed the blood of men.

ATHENA

Where is the place, then, where the killer's flight shall end?

CHORUS LEADER

A place where happiness is nevermore allowed.

ATHENA

Is he one? Do you blast him to this kind of flight?

CHORUS LEADER

Yes. He murdered his mother by deliberate choice.   425

ATHENA

Not by compulsion, nor fear of someone's wrath?

CHORUS LEADER

Where is the spur to justify man's matricide?

ATHENA

Here are two sides, and only half the argument.

CHORUS LEADER

He is unwilling to give or to accept an oath.

ATHENA

You wish to be called righteous rather than act right.   430

CHORUS LEADER

No. How so? From the wealth of your wisdom, explain.

ATHENA

I say, wrong must not win merely by oaths.

CHORUS LEADER

Examine him then yourself. Decide it, and be fair.

ATHENA

You would turn over authority in this case to me?

CHORUS LEADER

By all means. We respect your merits and whence they are
derived.° 435

ATHENA

Your turn, stranger. What will you say in answer? Speak,
tell me your country and your birth, what has befallen
you, then defend yourself against the censure of these;
if it is confidence in the right that makes you sit
guarding this image near my hearth, a suppliant 440
in the tradition of Ixion, sacrosanct.
Give me an answer which is plain to understand.

ORESTES

Lady Athena, first I will take the great worry
away that lies in these last words you spoke. I am
no suppliant, nor was it because I had a stain 445
upon my hand that I sat at your image. I
will give you a strong proof that what I say is true.
It is the law that the man of the bloody hand must speak
no word until, by action of an expert purifier,
the slaughter of a young animal has washed his blood away. 450
Long since, at the homes of others, I have been absolved
thus, both by running waters and by victims slain.
I count this scruple now out of the way. Learn next
with no delay where I am from. I am of Argos
and it is to my honor that you ask the name 455
of my father, Agamemnon, lord of seafarers,
and your companion when you made the Trojan city
of Ilium no city any more. He died
without honor when he came home. It was my mother
of the dark heart, who entangled him in intricate nets 460
and cut him down. The bath is witness to his death.
I was an exile in the time before this. I came back

and killed the woman who gave me birth. I don't deny it.
My father was dear, and this was vengeance for his blood.
Apollo shares responsibility for this.   465
He counterspurred my heart and told me of pains to come
if I should fail to act against the guilty ones.
This is my case. Decide if it be right or wrong.
I am in your hands. Where my fate falls, I shall accept.

ATHENA

The matter is too big for any mortal man   470
who thinks he can judge it. Nor yet do I have the right
to analyse cases of murder where wrath's edge
is sharp, and all the more since you have come, and clung
a clean and innocent suppliant against my doors.
You bring no harm to my city. I respect your rights.   475
Yet these, too, have their work. We cannot brush them aside,
and if this action so runs that they fail to win,
the venom of their resolution will return
to infect the soil, and sicken all my land to death.
Here is dilemma. Whether I let them stay or drive   480
them off, it is a hard course and will hurt. So, since
the burden of the case is here, and rests on me,
I shall select judges of manslaughter, and swear
them in, establish a court into all time to come.
Litigants, call your witnesses, have ready your proofs   485
as evidence under bond to keep this case secure.
I will pick the finest of my citizens, and come
back. They shall swear to make no judgment that is not
just, and make clear where in this action the truth lies.

(Exit Athena, to the side.)

CHORUS [*singing*]

STROPHE A

Here is overthrow of all   490
established laws,° if the claim
of this matricide shall stand

good, his crime be sustained.
Should this be, every man will find a way
to act at his own caprice;   495
over and over again in time
to come, parents shall await
the deathstroke at their children's hands.

We are the Angry Ones. But we
shall watch no more over works   500
of men, and so act. We shall
let loose indiscriminate death.
Man shall learn from man's lot, forejudge
the evils of his neighbor's case,
seek respite and escape from troubles:
pathetic prophet who consoles   505
with strengthless cures, in vain.

Nevermore let one who feels
the stroke of accident, uplift
his voice and make outcry, thus: 510
"Oh Justice!
Throned powers of the Furies, help!"
Such might be the pitiful cry
of some father, of the stricken
mother, their appeal. Now   515
the House of Justice has collapsed.

There are times when fear is good.
It must keep its watchful place
at the heart's controls. There is
advantage   520
in the wisdom won from pain.
If the city, if the man
rears a heart that nowhere goes

in fear, how shall such a one
any more respect the right?   525

Refuse the life of anarchy;
refuse the life devoted to
one master.
The in-between has the power
by a god's grant always, though   530
his ordinances vary.
I will speak in defense
of reason: for the very child
of vanity is Violence;
but out of health   535
in the heart is born the beloved
and the longed-for, prosperity.

All for all I tell you: show
respect for the altar of right.
You shall not   540
eye advantage, and kick
it over with foot of force.
Vengeance will be upon you.
The appointed end awaits.
Let someone see this and take   545
care, to mother and father,
and to the guest
in the gates welcomed, give all honor,
respecting their position.

The man who does right, free-willed, without constraint   550
shall not lose happiness
nor be wiped out with all his generation.
But the transgressor, I tell you, the bold man
who heaps up confusion of goods unjustly won,

at long last and perforce, when his ship toils   555
in the storm must strike his sail
midst the wreck of his rigging.

ANTISTROPHE D

He calls on those who hear not, caught inside
the hard wrestle of water.
The divinity laughs at the hot-hearted man,   560
the man who said "never to me," watches him
pinned in distress, unable to run free of the wave crests.
He had good luck in his life. Now
he smashes on the reef of right
and drowns, unwept and forgotten.   565

*(Athena reenters from the side, guiding eleven citizens
chosen as jurors° and attended by a herald.)*

ATHENA

Herald, make proclamation and gather in the host
assembled. Let the stabbing voice of the Etruscan
trumpet, blown to the full with mortal wind, crash out
its high call to all the mustered populace.
For in the filling of this deliberative assembly   570
it is best for all the city to be silent and learn
the measures I have laid down into the rest of time.
So too these litigants, that their case be fairly tried.

(Trumpet call. All take their places. Enter Apollo.)

CHORUS LEADER

My lord Apollo, rule within your own domain.
What in this matter has to do with you? Declare.   575

APOLLO

I come to testify. This man, by observed law,
came to me as suppliant, took his place by my hearth and hall,
and it was I who cleaned him of the stain of blood.
I have also come to help him win his case. I bear
responsibility for his mother's murder.

(To Athena.)

You   580

who know the rules, initiate the trial. Preside.

ATHENA   *(To the Furies.)*

I declare the trial opened. Yours is the first word.
For it must justly be the accuser who speaks first
and opens the case, and makes plain what the action is.

CHORUS LEADER

We are many, but we shall cut it short. You, then,   585
word against word answer our charges one by one.
Say first, did you kill your mother or did you not?

ORESTES

Yes, I killed her. There shall be no denial of that.

CHORUS LEADER

There are three falls in the match and one has gone to us.

ORESTES

So you say. But you have not even thrown your man.   590

CHORUS LEADER

So. Then how did you kill her? You are bound to say.

ORESTES

I do. With drawn sword in my hand I cut her throat.

CHORUS LEADER

By whose persuasion and advice did you do this?

ORESTES

By order of this god, here. So he testifies.

CHORUS LEADER

The prophet god guided you into this matricide?   595

ORESTES

Yes. I have never complained of this. I do not now.

CHORUS LEADER

When sentence seizes you, you will talk a different way.

ORESTES

I have no fear. My father will aid me from the grave.

CHORUS LEADER

Kill your mother, then put trust in a corpse! Trust on.

ORESTES

Yes. She was polluted twice over with disgrace.   600

CHORUS LEADER

Tell me how, and explain it to the judges here.

ORESTES

She murdered her husband, and thereby my father too.

CHORUS LEADER

Of this stain, death has set her free. But you still live.

ORESTES

While she lived, why did you not descend and drive her out?

CHORUS LEADER

The man she killed was not of blood congenital.   605

ORESTES

But do I then share with my mother a blood bond?

CHORUS LEADER

Yes, you butcher. How else could she have nursed you in
her womb? Do you forswear your mother's intimate blood?

ORESTES

Yours to bear witness now, Apollo, and expound
the case for me, if I was right to cut her down.   610
I will not deny I did this thing, because I did
do it. But was the bloodshed right or not? Decide
and answer. As you answer, I shall state my case.

APOLLO

    To you, judges, established by Athena in your power,
    I shall speak justly. I am a prophet, I shall not   615
    lie. Never, for man, woman, nor city, from my throne
    of prophecy have I spoken a word, except
    that which Zeus, father of Olympians, might command.
    This is justice. Recognize then how great its strength.
    I tell you, follow our father's will. For not even   620
    the oath that binds you is more strong than Zeus is strong.

CHORUS LEADER

    Then Zeus, as you say, authorized the oracle
    to this Orestes, stating he could wreak the death
    of his father on his mother, and it would have no force?

APOLLO

    It is not the same thing for a noble man to die,   625
    one honored with the king's staff given by the hand of god,
    and that by means of a woman, not with the far cast
    of fierce arrows, as an Amazon might have done,
    but in a way that you shall hear, O Pallas and you
    who sit in state to judge this action by your vote.   630

    He had come home from his campaigning. He had done
    better than worse, in the eyes of a fair judge. She lay
    in wait for him. It was the bath.° When he was at
    its edge, she hooded the robe on him, and in the blind
    and complex toils tangled her man, and chopped him down.   635

    That is the story of the death of a great man,
    revered in all men's sight, lord of the host of ships.
    I have called the woman what she was, so that the people
    whose duty it is to try this case may be inflamed.

CHORUS LEADER

    Zeus, by your story, gives first place to the father's death.   640
    Yet Zeus himself shackled elder Cronus, his own

father. Is this not contradiction? I testify,
judges, that this is being said in your hearing.

APOLLO

You foul animals, from whom the gods turn in disgust,
Zeus could undo shackles, such hurt can be made good,   645
and there is every kind of way to get out. But once
the dust has drained down all a man's blood, once the man
has died, there is no raising of him up again.
This is a thing for which my father never made
curative spells. All other states, without effort   650
of hard breath, he can completely rearrange.

CHORUS LEADER

See what it means to force acquittal of this man.
He has spilled his mother's blood upon the ground. Shall he
then be at home in Argos in his father's house?
What altars of the community shall he use? Is there   655
a brotherhood's lustration that will let him in?

APOLLO

I will tell you, and I will answer correctly. Watch.
The mother is no parent of that which is called
her child, but only nurse of the new-planted seed
that grows. The parent is he who mounts. A stranger she   660
preserves a stranger's seed, if no god interfere.
I will show you proof of what I have explained. There can
be a father without any mother. There she stands,
the living witness, daughter of Olympian Zeus,
she who was never fostered in the dark of the womb   665
yet such a child as no goddess could bring to birth.
In all else, Pallas, as I best may understand,
I shall make great your city and its populace.
So I have brought this man to sit beside the hearth
of your house, to be your true friend for the rest of time,   670
so you shall win him, goddess, to fight by your side,
and among men to come this shall stand a strong bond
that his and your own people's children shall be friends.

ATHENA

Shall I assume that enough has now been said, and tell
the judges to render what they believe a true verdict?   675

CHORUS LEADER

Every arrow we had has been shot now. We wait
on their decision, to see how the case has gone.

ATHENA

So then. How shall I act correctly in your eyes?

APOLLO

You have heard what you have heard, and as you cast your
    votes,
good friends, respect in your hearts the oath that you have
    sworn.   680

ATHENA

If it please you, men of Attica, hear my decree
now, as you judge this case, the first trial for bloodshed.
For Aegeus' population, this forevermore
shall be the ground where justices deliberate.
Here is the Hill of Ares, here the Amazons   685
encamped and built their shelters when they came in arms
in rage at Theseus, here they piled their rival towers
to rise, a new city against his city long ago,
and sacrificed for Ares. So this rock is named
from then the Hill of Ares. Here the reverence   690
of citizens, their fear and kindred do-no-wrong
shall hold by day and in the blessing of night alike
all while the people do not muddy their own laws
with foul infusions. But if bright water you stain
with mud, you nevermore will find it fit to drink.   695
No anarchy, no rule of a single master. Thus
I advise my citizens to govern and to grace,
and not to cast fear utterly from your city. What
man who fears nothing at all is ever righteous? Such
be your just terrors, and you may deserve and have   700

salvation for your citadel, your land's defense,
such as is nowhere else found among men, neither
among the Scythians, nor the land that Pelops held.
I establish this tribunal. It shall be untouched
by money making, grave but quick to wrath, watchful   705
to protect those who sleep, a sentry on the land.
These words I have spun out are for my citizens,
advice into the future. All must stand upright
now, take each man his ballot in his hand, think on
his oath, and make his judgment. For my word is said.   710

*(One by one, the eleven mortal jurors walk forward to place their
voting pebble into an urn: each time, Apollo or the Chorus speaks.)*

CHORUS LEADER
I give you counsel by no means to disregard
this company. We can be a weight to crush your land.

APOLLO
I speak too. I command you to fear, and not
make void the yield of oracles from Zeus and me.

CHORUS LEADER
You honor bloody actions where you have no right.   715
The oracles you give shall be no longer clean.

APOLLO
My father's purposes are twisted then. For he
was appealed to by Ixion, the first murderer.

CHORUS LEADER
Talk! But for my part, if I do not win the case,
I shall come back to this land and it will feel my weight.   720

APOLLO
Neither among the elder nor the younger gods
have you consideration. I shall win this suit.

CHORUS LEADER

Such was your action in the house of Pheres. Then
you beguiled the Fates to let mortals go free from death.

APOLLO

Is it not right to help the man who shows respect   725
and piety, above all when he stands in need?

CHORUS LEADER

You won the ancient goddesses over with wine
and so destroyed the orders of an elder time.

APOLLO

You shall not win the issue of this suit, but shall
be made to void your poison to no enemy's hurt.   730

CHORUS LEADER

Since you, a young god, would ride down my elder age,
I must stay here and listen to how the trial goes,
being yet uncertain to loose my anger on the state.

ATHENA

It is my task to render final judgment here.
This is a ballot for Orestes I shall cast.   735
There is no mother anywhere who gave me birth,
and, but for marriage, I am always for the male
with all my heart, and strongly on my father's side.
So, in a case where the wife has killed her husband, lord
of the house, I shall not value her death more highly than his.   740
And even if the votes are equal, Orestes is the winner.
You of the jurymen who have this duty assigned,
shake out the ballots from the vessels, with all speed.

ORESTES

Phoebus Apollo, what will the decision be?

CHORUS LEADER

Darkness of night, our mother, are you here to watch?   745

ORESTES

This is the end for me. The noose, or else the light.

CHORUS LEADER

Here our destruction, or our high duties confirmed.

APOLLO

Shake out the votes accurately, Athenian friends.
Be careful as you pick them up. Make no mistake.
In the lapse of judgment great disaster comes. The cast   750
of a single ballot can restore a house entire.

ATHENA

The man before us has escaped the charge of blood.
The ballots are in equal number for each side.

ORESTES

Pallas Athena, you have kept my house alive.
When I had lost the land of my fathers you gave me   755
a place to live. Among the Hellenes they shall say:
"A man of Argos lives again in the estates
of his father, all by grace of Pallas Athena, and
Apollo, and with them the all-ordaining god
the Savior"—who remembers my father's death, who looked   760
upon my mother's advocates, and rescues me.
I shall go home now, but before I go I swear
to this your country and to this your multitude
of people into all the bigness of time to be,
that never man who holds the helm of my state shall come   765
against your country in the ordered strength of spears,
but though I lie then in my grave, I still shall wreak
helpless bad luck and misadventure upon all
who step across the oath that I have sworn: their ways
disconsolate make, their crossings full of evil   770
augury, so they shall be sorry that they moved.
But while they keep the upright way, and hold in high
regard the city of Pallas, and align their spears
to fight beside her, I shall be their gracious spirit.

And so farewell, you and your city's populace. 775
May you outwrestle and overthrow all those who come
against you, to your safety and your spears' success.°

(*Exit Orestes to the side. Exit also Apollo.*)

CHORUS [*singing throughout this interchange with Athena, who speaks
in response*]
   Gods of the younger generation, you have ridden down
   the laws of the elder time, torn them out of my hands.
   I, disinherited, suffering, heavy with anger 780
   shall let loose on the land
   the vindictive poison
   dripping deadly out of my heart upon the ground;
   this from itself shall breed
   cancer, the leafless, the barren 785
   to strike, for the right, their low lands
   and drag its smear of mortal infection on the ground.
   What shall I do? Afflicted
   I am mocked by these people.
   I have borne what cannot 790
   be borne. Great the sorrows and the dishonor upon
   the sad daughters of Night.

ATHENA
   Listen to me. I would not have you be so grieved.
   For you have not been beaten. This was the result 795
   of a fair ballot which ended up even. You were not
   dishonored, but the luminous evidence of Zeus
   was there, and he who spoke the oracle was he
   who ordered Orestes so to act and not be hurt.
   Do not be angry any longer with this land 800
   nor bring the bulk of your hatred down on it; do not
   render it barren of fruit, nor spill the dripping rain
   of death in fierce and jagged lines to eat the seeds.
   In complete honesty I promise you a place
   of your own, deep hidden underground that is yours by right 805

where you shall sit on shining chairs beside the hearth
to accept devotions offered by your citizens.

CHORUS

Gods of the younger generation, you have ridden down
the laws of the elder time, torn them out of my hands.
I, disinherited, suffering, heavy with anger   810
shall let loose on the land
the vindictive poison
dripping deadly out of my heart upon the ground;
this from itself shall breed
cancer, the leafless, the barren   815
to strike, for the right, their low lands
and drag its smear of mortal infection on the ground.
What shall I do? Afflicted
I am mocked by these people.
I have borne what cannot   820
be borne. Great the sorrow and the dishonor upon
the sad daughters of Night.

ATHENA

No, not dishonored. You are goddesses. Do not
in too much anger make this place of mortal men   825
uninhabitable. I have Zeus behind me. Do
we need to speak of that? I am the only god
who knows the keys to where his thunderbolts are locked.
We do not need such, do we? Be reasonable
and do not from a reckless mouth cast on the land   830
spells that will ruin every thing which might bear fruit.
No. Put to sleep the bitter strength in the black wave
and live with me and share my pride of worship. Here
is a big land, and from it you shall win first fruits
in offerings for children and the marriage rite   835
for always. Then you will say my argument was good.

CHORUS

That they could treat me so!

I, the mind of the past, to be driven under the ground
outcast, like dirt!
The wind I breathe is fury and utter hate.   840
Earth, ah, Earth
what is this agony that crawls under my ribs?
Night, hear me, O Night,
mother. They have wiped me out   845
and the hard hands of the gods
and their treacheries have taken my old rights away.

ATHENA

I will bear your angers. You are elder born than I
and in that you are wiser far than I. Yet still
Zeus gave me too intelligence not to be despised.   850
If you go away into some land of foreigners,
I warn you, you will come to yearn for this country.
Time in forward flood shall ever grow more dignified
for the people of this city. And you, in your place
of eminence beside Erechtheus in his house   855
shall win from female and from male processionals
more than all lands of men beside could ever give.
Only in this place that I haunt do not inflict
your bloody stimulus to twist the inward hearts
of young men, raging in a fury not of wine,   860
nor, as if taking the heart from fighting cocks,
engraft among my citizens that spirit of war
that turns their battle fury inward on themselves.
No, let our wars range outward—may they range full fierce
and terrible, for those desiring high renown.   865
No true fighter I call the bird that fights at home.
Such life I offer you, and it is yours to take.
Do good, receive good, and be honored as the good
are honored. Share our country, the beloved of god.

CHORUS

That they could treat me so!   870
I, the mind of the past, to be driven under the ground

outcast, like dirt!
The wind I breathe is fury and utter hate.
Earth, ah, Earth
what is this agony that crawls under my ribs?   875
Night, hear me, O Night,
mother. They have wiped me out
and the hard hands of the gods
and their treacheries have taken my old rights away.   880

ATHENA

I will not weary of telling you all the good things
I offer, so that you can never say that you,
an elder god, were driven unfriended from the land
by me in my youth, and by my mortal citizens.
But if you hold Persuasion has her sacred place   885
of worship, in the sweet beguilement of my voice,
then you might stay with us. But if you wish to stay
then it would not be justice to inflict your rage
upon this city, your resentment or bad luck
to armies. You can be landholders in this country   890
if you will, in all justice, with full privilege.

CHORUS LEADER [*speaking*]

Lady Athena, what is this place you say is mine?

ATHENA

A place free of all grief and pain. Take it for yours.

CHORUS LEADER

If I do take it, shall I have some definite powers?

ATHENA

No household shall be prosperous without your will.   895

CHORUS LEADER

You will do this? You will really let me be so strong?

ATHENA

So we shall straighten the lives of all who worship us.

CHORUS LEADER

You guarantee such honor for the rest of time?

ATHENA

I have no need to promise what I cannot do.

CHORUS LEADER

I think you will have your way with me. My hate is going.   900

ATHENA

Stay here, then, in this land, and gain others too as friends.

CHORUS LEADER

I will put a spell upon the land. What shall it be?

ATHENA

Something that has no traffic with evil success.
Let it come out of the ground, out of the sea's water,
and from the high air make the waft of gentle gales   905
wash over the country in full sunlight, and the seed
and stream of the soil's yield and of the grazing beasts
be strong and never fail our people as time goes,
and make the human seed be kept alive. Make more
the issue of those who worship more your ways, for as   910
the gardener works in love, so love I best of all
the unblighted generation of these upright men.
All such is yours for granting. In the speech and show
and pride of battle, I myself shall not endure
this city's eclipse in the estimation of mankind.   915

CHORUS [*singing throughout the following interchange with Athena,
who chants in response*]

STROPHE A

I accept this home at Athena's side.
I shall not forget the cause
of this city, which Zeus all powerful and Ares
rule, stronghold of divinities,
glory of Hellene gods, their guarded altar.   920
So with forecast of good

I sing this prayer for them
that the sun's bright magnificence shall break out wave
on wave of all the happiness   925
life can give, across their land.

ATHENA

Here are my actions. In all goodwill
toward these citizens I establish in power
these great divinities, difficult to soften.
To them is given the handling entire   930
of men's lives. That man
who has felt the full weight of their hands°
takes the strokes of life, knows not whence, not why,
for crimes wreaked in past generations
drag him before these powers. Loud his voice   935
but the silent doom
hates hard, and breaks him to dust.

CHORUS

ANTISTROPHE A

Let there blow no wind that wrecks the trees.
I pronounce words of grace.
Nor blaze of heat blind the blossoms of grown plants, nor   940
cross the circles of its right
place. Let no barren deadly sickness creep and kill.
May flocks fatten. Earth be kind
to them, with double fold of fruit   945
in time appointed for its yielding. Secret child
of Earth, her hidden wealth, bestow
blessing and surprise of gods.

ATHENA

Strong guard of our city, hear you these
and what they portend? Fury is a high queen   950
of strength even among the immortal gods
and the undergods, and for humankind
they accomplish their work, absolute, clear:

for some, singing; for some, life dimmed
in tears; theirs the disposition.   955

CHORUS

Death of manhood cut down
before its prime I forbid:
girls' grace and glory find
men to live life with them.
Grant, you who have the power.   960
And O, steering spirits of law,
goddesses of Destiny,
sisters from my mother, hear;
in all houses implicated,
in all time heavy of hand   965
on whom your just arrest falls,
most august among goddesses.

ATHENA

It is my glory to hear how these
generosities
are given my land. I admire the eyes   970
of Persuasion, who guided the speech of my mouth
toward these, when they were reluctant and wild.
Zeus, who guides men's speech in councils, was too
strong; and my ambition
for good wins out in the whole issue.   975

CHORUS

This my prayer: civil war
fattening on men's ruin shall
not thunder in our city. Let
not the dry dust that drinks
the black blood of citizens   980
through passion for revenge
and bloodshed for bloodshed

be given our state to prey upon.
Let them render grace for grace.
Let love be their common will;   985
let them hate with single heart.
Much wrong in the world thereby is healed.

ATHENA

Are they taking thought to discover that road
where speech goes straight?
In the fearsome look of the faces of these   990
I see great good for our citizens.
While with goodwill you hold in high honor
these Kindly Spirits, their will shall be good, as you steer
your city, your land
on an upright course clear through to the end.   995

CHORUS
STROPHE C

Farewell, farewell. High destiny shall be yours
by right. Farewell, citizens
seated near the throne of Zeus,
beloved by the Maiden he loves,
civilized as years go by,   1000
sheltered under Athena's wings,
revered in her father's sight.

ATHENA

Goddesses, farewell. Mine to lead, as these
attend us, to where
by the sacred light new chambers are given.   1005
Go then. Sped by majestic sacrifice
from these, plunge beneath the ground. There hold
off what might hurt the land; pour in
the city's advantage, success in the end.
You, children of Cranaus, you who keep   1010
the citadel, guide these guests of the state.

For good things given,
your hearts' desire be for good to return.

CHORUS

Farewell and again farewell, words spoken twice over,
all who by this citadel,   1015
mortal men, spirits divine,
hold the city of Pallas, grace
this my guestship in your land.
Life will give you no regrets.   1020

(A second Chorus, of women of Attica, begins to enter, from the side.)

ATHENA [*now speaking*]

Well said. I assent to all the burden of your prayers,
and by the light of flaring torches now attend
your passage to the deep and subterranean hold,
as by us walk those women whose high privilege
it is to guard my image. Flower of all the land   1025
of Theseus, let them issue now, grave companies,
maidens, wives, elder women, in processional.°
In the investiture of purple-stained robes
dignify them, and let the torchlight go before
so that the kindly company of these within   1030
our ground may shine in the future of strong men to come.

(The first Chorus begin to replace their black
robes with reddish-purple ones.)

SECOND CHORUS [*singing*]

STROPHE A

Home, home, O high, O aspiring
Daughters of Night, aged children, in kindly processional.
Bless them, all here, with words of good omen.   1035

ANTISTROPHE A

In the primeval dark of earth-hollows

held in high veneration with rights sacrificial
bless them, all people, with words of good omen.

STROPHE B

Wish favor, wish justice for this land,   1040
and follow, august goddesses, flushed in the flamesprung
torchlight, delighting in your journey.
Singing all follow our footsteps.

ANTISTROPHE B

There shall be peace forever between these people
of Pallas and their guests. Zeus the all-seeing   1045
joined with Destiny to confirm it.
Singing all follow our footsteps.

(Everybody departs, in procession.)

PROTEUS
(FRAGMENTS)

Translated by MARK GRIFFITH

PROTEUS (SATYR-PLAY)

Characters   PROTEUS (king of Egypt, and/or shape-changing
"Old Man of the Sea")
EIDO (Eidothea), his daughter
MENELAUS?
HELEN?
CHORUS of Satyrs, with their father
Papposilenus

Scene: *Egypt, or perhaps an island off the coast.*

Almost nothing is known for certain about this, the final play
of the *Oresteia* tetralogy, since only two complete lines of it survive in quotation (Aeschylus fragment 210), and these give us
no clue about the plot:

> . . . a wretched, miserable pigeon, trying to feed
> after its ribs have been smashed by the fans winnowing the
>   grain.

A few other individual words quoted are concerned largely
with items of food and do not tell us much about the plot; but
we do know something about the cast of characters. Most scholars have concluded that the drama involved Menelaus' journey
homeward after the capture of Troy, along the lines of book 4
of the *Odyssey*, with Menelaus encountering the Old Man of the
Sea and forcing him to reveal the truth about his future travels.

Alternatively, Aeschylus may have followed the version of
the sixth-century lyric poet Stesichorus, whose *Palinode* (now

largely lost) famously asserted that Helen never actually sailed to Troy at all with Paris, but spent the duration of the Trojan War in Egypt under the benevolent supervision of King Proteus—while Paris enjoyed merely a phantom, and it was for this that the Trojan War was fought. In these "revisionist" versions, Menelaus only comes to realize the truth about Helen when he arrives (usually by shipwreck) in Egypt and finds his true wife waiting for him there. This version (of which hints may be detected in *Agamemnon*) is discussed at length by Herodotus (book 2) and is followed by Euripides in his *Helen*.

TEXTUAL NOTES

(The line numbers indicated are in some cases only approximate.)

AGAMEMNON

70. Text uncertain.

84. Perhaps Clytaemestra has entered silently at this point: scholars disagree.

144. Text and interpretation uncertain.

216. Text uncertain: some editors emend to read, "it is right for them to yearn furiously for the maiden's blood."

256-57. It is unclear whether the chorus mean Clytaemestra, or themselves. When exactly Clytaemestra enters is uncertain. Some scholars think that she enters silently as early as line 84.

287. Perhaps one or more lines are missing at this point.

470. Text uncertain: possibly "crash on the towering mountains."

489-500. The manuscripts (and a few editors) assign these lines to Clytaemestra, not the chorus.

570-75. Some scholars suggest that these lines must be put into a different order and that several lines are missing here.

804. Text very uncertain; some words may be missing.

934. Text uncertain. Possibly, "I, if anyone, would have known and spoken this duty."

985. Text uncertain.

1001-7. Some words seem to be missing here, and the text is very uncertain.

1090-92. Text very uncertain.

1284. This line is transposed here (from its position between 1289 and 1290 in the manuscripts) by almost all modern editors.

1359. Text uncertain.

1447. Exact reading uncertain, but the reference to a "spicy side dish" is definite.

1474. The text is defective here.

1499. Exact text and interpretation are disputed.

1527. Exact text uncertain, but the general sense is clear.

1650–54. The assignment of speakers for each of these lines is disputed.

1657. Text uncertain.

1662. Text uncertain.

THE LIBATION BEARERS

1–9. These lines are supplied from references in other Greek authors, including Aristophanes' *Frogs*, as separate quotations (1–3, 4–5a, 5b, 6–7, 8–9). The first page of the only existing manuscript of our play is missing, and it is unknown exactly how many lines have been lost or how many lines may intervene between these separate quotations.

92. The ordering of lines 92–99 is disputed. The translation here follows the order in the manuscript.

123. This line is transmitted by the manuscript as line 165 and is transposed here by modern scholars.

197. Text uncertain: possibly, "but I could know for sure to throw this strand . . ."

227–30. Scholars disagree on the proper sequence of these lines, and one line may be missing.

245. "Your" is an emendation; the manuscript reading is "be on my side"; some editors write "on our side." Some scholars assign lines 244–45 to Orestes rather than Electra.

255–263. Some editors assign these lines to Electra rather than Orestes.

285–90. The text of these lines is very uncertain.

314–509. In this long ritualized invocation of Agamemnon's spirit, the distribution of stanzas or individual verses between the chorus, Orestes, and Electra is not reliably recorded in the manuscript, and sometimes the correct assignment remains uncertain.

360. A possible alternative reading is, "you were king on earth when you lived."

375–79. Reading and interpretation very uncertain; a phrase may have dropped out.

386. Text uncertain.

415–18. Reading and sense extremely uncertain.

482. Text very uncertain, and some syllables are missing in the manuscript. Different supplements have been proposed by various editors. Some scholars have restored the text to read, "to bring death on Aegisthus and find myself a husband."

503–9. Distribution of speakers uncertain (see note on 314–509): some editors give 503–4 to Orestes, 505–7 to Electra, 508–9 to Orestes. Others delete 505–7 completely and assign 508–9 to Electra.

517. Reading uncertain.

534. Reading and sense very uncertain; some editors emend to read, "This vision would not be empty."

628. Text uncertain.

727. Reading and sense very uncertain.

785–86. Text very uncertain.

803. Two or three words are missing in the manuscript at this point.

831–36. The precise reading is uncertain in several places here, but the general sense is not in doubt.

929. The manuscript seems to assign this line ("indeed, this terror . . . clearly") to Orestes; some modern scholars prefer to attribute it to Clytaemestra.

THE EUMENIDES

85–87. Some scholars transpose these lines to before line 64.

104–5. Most editors delete line 104 ("Eyes . . . brain"); some delete 105 as well.

188. The exact reading and translation are uncertain; but the general sense is not in doubt.

352. One line appears to be missing after this.

360-61. The text and meaning of these two lines are very uncertain.

381. Some editors adopt here the emendation, "For we alone" (*monai*), instead of the manuscript's "all holds" (*menei*).

404. After this line, the manuscripts contain a line that says, "after yoking this chariot of mine to speedy horses." Editors delete this as it contradicts the previous two lines. Presumably the line was inserted for an alternative mode of entry to the stage for Athena in a later production.

435. The precise reading here is uncertain.

491. The manuscripts here read "overthrow of new laws." Most editors have adopted some kind of emendation, since "new" appears to mean the opposite of what is required by the context. In the first edition, Lattimore translated as "overthrow of all the young laws."

565. Scholars disagree as to whether Athena appoints eleven or twelve human jurors. Since in the end her vote is counted along with theirs and the total of votes is then equal (711-53), it appears that they should be an odd number.

632-33. Some scholars have suggested that a line may be missing here.

775-77. Some scholars assign these lines to Apollo rather than to Orestes.

932. Text uncertain.

1027. Some lines may be missing here. Perhaps in them the Erinyes were called "Eumenides" (the name, which gives this play its title, does not occur anywhere in the extant text).

GLOSSARY

Achaeans: ancient name (common in Homer) for the Greeks who besieged and sacked Troy; also called Argives and Danaans.

Acheron: a river or lake in the underworld across which the dead are ferried.

Aegeus: father of Theseus; king of Athens.

Aegisthus: sole surviving son of Thyestes, and thus cousin of Agamemnon; lover, and eventually husband, of Clytaemestra.

Aegyplanctus: a mountain of unknown location.

Agamemnon: son of Atreus; brother of Menelaus and husband of Clytaemestra; father of Iphigeneia, Electra, and Orestes. King of Argos (Mycenae) and leader of the Greek expedition against Troy.

Alcmene: mother of Heracles.

Alexander: another name for Paris, prince of Troy, son of Priam and Hecuba. He abducted Helen from Menelaus' home.

Althaea: daughter of Thestius and mother of Meleager.

Amazon: the Amazons, descendants of Ares, were a race of militaristic man-hating women thought to live in northern Anatolia on the coast of the Black Sea. They invaded Attica after Theseus abducted their queen Antiope, but were eventually defeated.

Angry Ones: the Furies.

Apian land: the Peloponnesus, named for the seer Apis, an early king of Argos.

Apollo: son of Zeus and Leto; god of healing, purification, and prophecy. (Also known as Loxias and Phoebus.) His main oracular shrine was at Delphi.

Arachnus: a mountain in the northern Peloponnese on the way from Epidaurus to Argos.

Areopagus: *see* Ares

Ares: the god of war; father of the Amazons. The Hill of Ares (Areopagus) near the Acropolis was the place where the Athenian homicide court, comprised of former archons, met to hear cases.

Argives: the inhabitants of Argos; more generally, a term used collectively (like Achaeans or Danaans) by Homer and other poets to refer to the Greeks who besieged and sacked Troy.

Argolis: the region in the eastern part of the Peloponnese in which the city of Argos is located.

Argos: a city in the Peloponnese located in the southern region of the Argive plain; home of Agamemnon. The name is often used interchangeably with Mycenae, which was nearby and in the classical period barely existed as a town.

Arian: Arians (or Aryans), later known as the Medes, were the people of what is now the northwest of Iran: roughly equivalent to "Persian" in the Athenian view.

Artemis: daughter of Zeus; sister of Apollo; the virgin goddess of the hunt and of all young animals and unmarried girls.

Asclepius: son of Apollo and Coronis; supremely talented doctor, able even to cure the dead and bring them back to life—for which Zeus destroyed him with a thunderbolt.

Asopus: a river in Boeotia north of Mount Cithaeron.

Athena: daughter of Zeus, born from his head after he swallowed the goddess Metis ("Intelligence"), whom he had impregnated. Athena is the patron goddess of Athens, honored as maiden, warrior, and city protector.

Athens: main city in the plain of Attica in eastern Greece.

Athos: a mountain in Macedonia (northern Greece) on the Athos Peninsula.

Atreidae: the two sons of Atreus, Agamemnon and Menelaus.

Atreus: brother of Thyestes; father of Agamemnon and Menelaus.

Attica: a large region in southeast Greece dominated and ruled by Athens.

Aulis: a small town on the coast of Boeotia almost opposite Chalcis (Euboea). It was here that the Greek army assembled before sailing to Troy.

Bacchanals: celebrations of Dionysus by Bacchants, the female followers of the god.

battle god: Ares.

Bromius: epithet of Dionysus meaning "the thunderer." Dionysus resided at Delphi during the winter months when Apollo was away.

Calchas: the most important Greek seer who accompanied the army to Troy.

Cassandra: daughter of Priam, then, after Troy was captured, the concubine of Agamemnon. Apollo endowed her with the gift of prophecy but cursed her to be disbelieved by all.

Chalcis: a city on the island of Euboea facing Aulis.

Cilissa: literally, "woman/slave from Cilicia" (a region on the southern coast of what is now Turkey); nurse of Orestes.

Cissian: Cissia was the region in Persia around Susa, the capital city of Elam (modern-day Khuzestan in southwest Iran).

Cithaeron: a mountain in central Greece; Boeotia is to its north, Attica to its south.

Clytaemestra: daughter of Tyndareus; sister of Helen; wife of Agamemnon; mother of Iphigenia, Electra, and Orestes; lover of Aegisthus. Also written Clytemnestra.

Cocytus: a river in the underworld which flows into Acheron.

Corycian Rock: cave on Mount Parnassus sacred to Pan.

Cranaus: according to legend the second king of Athens.

Crete: large island to the southeast of mainland Greece.

Cronus: father of Zeus and other Olympian gods; one of the Titans. When Zeus and the younger generation of gods defeated the Titans, Cronus was imprisoned forever in Tartarus, the lowest level of Hades.

Cypris: another name for Aphrodite. The island Cyprus, located in the eastern Mediterranean to the southeast of modern-day Turkey, was sacred to her.

Danaans: One of the terms (along with Achaeans and Argives) used generally by Homer and other poets to refer to the Greeks who besieged and sacked Troy.

Daulian: Daulis was a city in Phocis.

Delos: island in the center of the ring of islands known as the Cyclades in the Aegean Sea; birthplace of Apollo and Artemis.

Delphus: son of Poseidon and Melantho; a legendary early king of Delphi after whom the region is named.

Dog Star: also called Sirius; its appearance in the sky signaled the hottest time of summer in August.

Earth (Queen): Gaia, mother/grandmother of all the gods and goddesses.

Eido: daughter of Proteus (abbreviated form of Eidothea). The word in Greek also means "image, phantom."

Electra: daughter of Clytaemestra and Agamemnon; sister of Orestes and Iphigenia.

Erechtheus: legendary king of Athens.

Eumenides: *see* Kindly Ones

Euripus: the straits separating Euboea from Boeotia, between Calchis and Aulis.

Fates: three daughters of Zeus and Themis or of Night; often imagined as spinning out portions to each human being.

Fury: a female avenging spirit especially concerned with bloodguilt, but also with other violations of sacred duties and taboos. The Furies are the children of Night. The Greek word is *Erinys*, plural *Erinyes*.

Geryon: three-bodied giant killed by Heracles.

Gorgons: three female monsters, sisters, so hideous that whoever looked upon them was turned to stone. The hero Perseus cut off the head of the mortal sister (Medusa) and was pursued by her immortal sisters.

Gorgopis: a lake of unknown location.

Hades: brother of Zeus and other Olympian gods; ruler over the underworld. The name is often used to mean the underworld itself, like "Pit."

Helen: daughter of Zeus/Tyndareus and Leda; sister of Clytaemestra; wife of Menelaus; eloped to Troy with Paris. Helen is often cited as the cause of the Trojan War. Her name in Greek (Helenê) sounds like "to kill" or "capture" (*helein*): hence "Hell to men," etc.

Hellas, Hellene: Greece, a Greek.

Hephaestus: the god of fire and metalwork.

Hermaean horn: a promontory on the island of Lemnos named for Hermes.

Hermes: son of Zeus and Maia; god of travel, contests, stealth, and heralds. He escorts the souls of the dead to the underworld.

Hill of Ares: the Areopagus. *See also* Ares

Ida: a mountain located to the southeast of Troy.

Ilium: another name for Troy, a wealthy city in northwest Anatolia (modern Turkey).

Inachus: river and river god of the Argive plain; father of Io and ancestor of the Argive royal family.

Iphigeneia: eldest daughter of Agamemnon and Clytaemestra; apparently sacrificed at the command of Artemis when the Greek fleet was blocked by bad sailing weather on the shores of Aulis. (In most versions, she is saved at the last minute by Artemis.) Also written Iphigenia.

Itys: son of Procne; killed by his mother to avenge her husband Tereus' rape of her sister Philomela. Procne was turned into a nightingale, a bird associated with lament.

Ixion: the first human to commit kin murder (he killed his father-in-law). He was refused purification by men and gods but was eventually pitied by Zeus, who welcomed him to Olympus—where he tried to rape Hera. He was finally punished by spending eternity in Hades tied to a turning wheel.

Kindly Ones: a euphemistic term for the Furies. (The name "Eumenides" is not actually found in our text of that play, though other words of similar meaning are applied to the Furies in the later scenes).

Lady Earth: Gaia, mother of the gods.

Leda: wife of Tyndareus; mother of Clytaemestra and Helen (the latter, from Zeus).

Lemnian: according to legend, the women of the island of Lemnos did not honor Aphrodite, so she gave them a foul smell. Repulsed, their husbands captured and had sex with the women from nearby Thrace. The Lemnian women were offended and murdered all their male relatives.

Lemnos: an island in the northeast Aegean Sea.

Leto: mother (with Zeus) of Apollo and Artemis.

Libyan: Libya was a region of North Africa, containing the cities of Cyrene and Carthage.

Loxias: epithet of Apollo often used in place of his name; the name means "crooked" and may come from the riddling nature of Apollo's oracles.

Lycian: Lycia was a region in southwest Anatolia (modern-day Turkey). The Lycians were allies of the Trojans against the Greeks in the Trojan War.

Macistus: a region in central Euboea.

Maia: daughter of Atlas; one of the Pleiades; mother of Hermes.

Menelaus: son of Atreus; brother of Agamemnon; husband of Helen.

Messapion: a mountain in Euboea, a region in central Greece.

Minos: son of Zeus and Europa; king of Crete

Night: primeval goddess, sometimes regarded as mother of the (fatherless) Furies.

Nisus: king of Megara; father of Scylla. He had an immortality-conferring lock of hair, which his daughter, in love with Minos, cut off when Minos was besieging Megara.

North Wind: called Boreas in Greek, he brings cold wind from Thrace.

Odysseus: a leader in the Greek army at Troy renowned for his intelligence and guile, and for his loyalty to Agamemnon.

Olympian gods: the twelve main Greek gods (Aphrodite, Apollo, Ares, Artemis, Athena, Demeter, Dionysus, Hephaestus, Hera, Hermes, Poseidon, Zeus) who have their home on Mount Olympus.

Orestes: son of Agamemnon and Clytaemestra; brother of Electra and Iphigeneia.

Orpheus: renowned singer whose voice could move objects and enchant animals.

Pallas: Athena.

Pan: a pastoral and woodland divinity; god of shepherds and the hunting of small animals.

Paris: another name for Alexander, prince of Troy, son of Priam; he abducted Helen from Menelaus' home.

Parnassus (Parnassian): a mountain in the region of Phocis in central Greece that towers over Delphi.

Pelops (Pelopidae): father of Atreus and Thyestes; son of Tantalus. The Pelopidae are the dynastic family ruling Argos, descendants of Pelops.

Pentheus: son of Agave and Echion; grandson of Cadmus. As king of Thebes, he resisted Dionysus' worship, and was torn limb from limb by his mother and other women of Thebes who were maddened by the god.

Persephone: daughter of Demeter and Zeus; queen of the underworld, wife of Hades. Also known as Kore (Daughter, Girl).

Perseus: son of Zeus and Danae; ordered by Polydectes, the king of Seriphus, to get the head of Medusa (*see* Gorgons); legendary founder of Mycenae.

Pheres: father of Admetus; founder and king of Pherae in Thessaly. Apollo, punished by Zeus for killing the Cyclopes in response to Zeus' slaying of Asclepius, had to spend a year in servitude to Admetus. In appreciation for his kind treatment Apollo convinced the Fates to allow Admetus to avoid death if he could find another to die in his place. Alcestis, Admetus' wife, offered herself. This is the subject of Euripides' *Alcestis*.

Phineus: blind king of Thrace who was tormented by Harpies, disgusting winged female creatures who kept snatching his food away or befouling it.

Phlegraean: the plain of Phlegra was the site of the final battle between the gods and the Giants. Some ancient geographers located it in Campania (Italy) near Cumae.

Phocis (Phocian): a region in central Greece, near Delphi.

Phoebe: one of the Titans; grandmother (through Leto) of Apollo and Artemis.

Phoebus: epithet of Apollo meaning "bright."

Pit: Hades (i.e., the underworld).

Pleiades: A constellation of stars visible during the sailing season (mid-May to early November); named for the seven daughters of Atlas and Pleione.

Pleisthenes: either a son of Pelops and brother of Atreus and Thyestes, or the father of Thyestes and Atreus, or a son of Atreus.

Pleistus: river that flows from Mount Parnassus into the Corinthian Gulf.

Poseidon: brother of Zeus; father of Delphus; god of the sea, of horses, and of earthquakes; he once shared the Delphic oracle with Earth.

Priam: king of Troy, father of Cassandra and many other daughters and sons.

Proteus: a shape-shifting sea-god, prophet and sage, who lived on the island of Pharos, off the coast of Egypt; also a mythical king of Egypt during the time of the Trojan War.

Pylades: son of Strophius; cousin and comrade of Orestes. (In several versions, he marries Electra.)

Pythian: *see* Pytho. The Pythian King is Apollo. The Pythia is the priestess at Apollo's oracular shrine at Delphi.

Pytho: Another name for Delphi; the name Pytho comes from the serpent Python, killed by Apollo.

Saronic strait: the water between the coast of Epidaurus (Argolid) and Aegina in southeastern Greece.

Scamandrus: a river on the Trojan plain.

Scylla: a six-headed female monster with the voice of a puppy who lived in a cave opposite Charybdis (a giant whirlpool) and fed on passing sailors. Encountered by Odysseus in the *Odyssey*.

Scythian: Scythia was the name given to the wild lands along the Black Sea to the northeast of mainland Greece (modern-day Bulgaria, Romania, Ukraine). The Scythians were noted for their savagery, nomadism, and archery.

Simoeis: a river on the Trojan plain.

Strophius: king of Phocis; half-brother of Agamemnon and Menelaus; father of Pylades.

Strymon: a large river in Thrace.

Sun: sometimes regarded as a personified deity (called Helios).

Syria: a region in the Levant, roughly equivalent to modern-day Syria, Palestine, and Lebanon; the adjective "Syrian" often means nothing more than "eastern" or "Oriental."

Tantalus: father of Pelops; grandfather of Atreus and great-grandfather of Agamemnon. He cut up and tried to feed Pelops to the gods to test their omniscience, and was punished with eternal suffering in the underworld.

Teucrus: ancestor of the Trojan kings.

Themis: daughter of Earth (Gaia) and Sky (Uranus); divine personification of right, propriety, natural law.

Theseus: son of Aegeus (or Poseidon) and Aethra; father of Demophon and Acamas; king of Athens.

Thestius: father of Althaea; king of Pleuron, a city in Aetolia.

Thracian: ancient Thrace was a large region, largely non-Greek, to the northeast of Greece (covering what is now northeastern Greece, southeastern Bulgaria, and northwest Turkey).

Thyestes: brother of Atreus; father of Aegisthus.

Titans: the sons and daughters of Gaia and Uranus; the generation preceding the Olympian gods. Their leader was Chronus, the father of Zeus.

Triton: lake in Libya from which Athena may have been born.

Trojans: the people of Troy (also called Ilium) who fought against the Greeks.

Troy: wealthy city in northwest Anatolia (modern-day Turkey) sacked by Agamemnon and the Greeks; also called Ilium.

Tyndareus: husband of Leda; father of Clytaemestra and presumptive
father of Helen.

war god: Ares.

Zeus: king of the gods; god of guests and hospitality, and also of the
thunderbolt; symbolic "father" of gods and humans; also "savior," the
god to whom the third libation of wine was traditionally poured when
making a prayer.